THE ULTIMATE
NINJA SMOOTHIE
RECIPE BOOK FOR EVERYONE

COPYRIGHT

INTRODUCTION

Welcome to The Ultimate Ninja Smoothie Recipe Book, your guide to 100 mouth-watering smoothie recipes crafted for your Ninja blender. This book is designed for health enthusiasts, fitness fanatics, and anyone looking to enjoy delicious, nutrient-rich smoothies. With your Ninja blender's power and precision, you can easily transform a variety of ingredients into tasty, nutritious beverages.

Our comprehensive recipe collection caters to all tastes and dietary needs, including:

- Energizing breakfast smoothies for a vibrant start to your day.
- Fruit-based blends for a healthy, sweet treat.
- Nutrient-packed green smoothies for a vitamin boost.
- Protein-rich post-workout smoothies to support muscle recovery.
- Immunity-boosting concoctions for a stronger defense system.
- Guilt-free decadent dessert smoothies.
- Detoxifying smoothies for body cleansing and well-being.
- Customizable recipes with alternative ingredients for personal preferences.

Additionally, you'll find tips for maximizing your Ninja blender's performance, including ingredient selection, layering techniques, and smoothie storage methods. This guide invites you to explore and experiment with smoothies, aligning your creations with your wellness goals. So, get your blender ready and join us in blending your way to health and happiness with "The Ultimate Ninja Smoothie Recipe Book.

HOW TO MAKE SMOOTHIE IN NINJA BLENDER

Making a smoothie in a Ninja blender is a simple and straightforward process. Follow these easy steps to create a delicious and nutritious smoothie in no time:

- **Choose your ingredients:** Begin by selecting the fruits, vegetables, and other ingredients you'd like to include in your smoothie. You can use fresh or frozen produce, depending on your preference and availability. Consider incorporating leafy greens, such as spinach or kale, for added nutrients. You can also add in yogurt, milk, or a milk alternative, such as almond or soy milk, for creaminess.

- **Prepare your ingredients:** Wash and chop your fruits and vegetables into smaller pieces to make blending easier. If you're using frozen fruits, there's no need to thaw them; they'll help create a thicker, frostier consistency.

- **Add ingredients to the blender:** Start by adding the softer ingredients, such as fresh fruits or leafy greens, to the bottom of the Ninja blender. This will help the blender process the ingredients more efficiently. Next, add any frozen fruits, vegetables, or ice cubes. Finally, pour in your chosen liquid (water, juice, milk, or milk alternative) and any additional ingredients, such as nuts, seeds, protein powder, or sweeteners.

- **Blend your smoothie:** Secure the blender lid and start blending on low speed. Gradually increase the speed as needed to thoroughly blend the ingredients. Most Ninja blenders have a "smoothie" setting, which is designed to create the perfect consistency. Blend until your smoothie reaches your desired texture, stopping to scrape down the sides of the blender with a spatula if necessary.

- **Taste and adjust:** Give your smoothie a taste and adjust the flavors or consistency as needed. You may want to add more sweetener, liquid, or other ingredients to achieve your desired taste and texture.

- **Serve and enjoy:** Once your smoothie is ready, pour it into a glass or a to-go container and enjoy immediately. Smoothies are best consumed fresh, but you can also store them in the refrigerator for up to 24 hours in a sealed container.

TABLE OF CONTENT

1. APPLE CIDER SMOOTHIE

An apple cider smoothie is a healthy beverage made by blending fresh apple cider, creamy Greek yogurt, and apple chunks. This smoothie is rich in antioxidants, vitamins, and minerals that are beneficial to overall health.

Drinking an apple cider smoothie in the morning can provide a boost of energy and help jumpstart metabolism, making it a perfect breakfast choice. Moreover, the presence of fiber in the smoothie may assist with digestion and provide a sense of satiety that lasts all day.

Apple cider smoothies are ideal for individuals looking for a low-calorie, nutrient-dense beverage. They are particularly suitable for those on a weight loss or weight maintenance diet, as they can help curb hunger and provide essential nutrients without adding excessive calories.

Prep Time: 5 Mins

Cook Time: 0 Mins

Total Time: 5 Mins

Servings: 2

Ingredients

- 1 cup of Greek yogurt
- Enough ice to fill the blender ¾ full
- 2 tbsp Tate+Lyle® Honey Granules (or honey to sweeten)
- 2 cups of fresh apple cider
- 1 apple, cored and cut into chunks
- ½ tspground cinnamon

Instructions

1. In the canister of a blender, combine the apple cider, Greek yogurt, apple chunks, Tate+Lyle® Honey Granules (or honey), and ground cinnamon.
2. Add enough ice to fill the blender about 3/4 full.
3. Keep blending the mixture until it achieves the texture that you prefer.
4. Pour the smoothie into two tall glasses.
5. Top with a slice of apple (if desired).
6. Serve the smoothie immediately and enjoy!

2. APPLE CINNAMON SMOOTHIE

An Apple Cinnamon Smoothie is a delicious and healthy drink that is perfect for any time of day. Crafted from crisp apples, cinnamon, and other wholesome components, this smoothie is an excellent selection for those seeking to enhance their health and wellness.

A significant advantage of this smoothie is its high level of antioxidants, which have been shown to decrease inflammation and safeguard against persistent illnesses. Apples, in particular, are high in fiber and vitamins C and K, while cinnamon is known for its anti-inflammatory and blood sugar-regulating properties.

This smoothie is best consumed in the morning or as a mid-day snack, as it can help to boost energy levels and reduce hunger cravings. In addition, this smoothie is an ideal option for individuals who aim to manage or shed weight since it is low in calories and high in essential nutrients.

Prep Time: 10 Mins

Cook Time: 0 Mins

Total Time: 10 Mins

Servings: 2

Ingredients

- 1 1/2 tsp ground cinnamon
- 1 tbsp maple syrup
- 1 tbsp almond butter
- 1 apple, peeled, cored and chopped
- 1 tspvanilla
- 1/2 cup of plain Greek yogurt
- 1/2 cup of milk of your choice
- 1/3 cup of rolled oats, gluten-free if necessary
- 1 large frozen banana, chopped

Instructions

1. Add all the ingredients into a blender.
2. Blend until smooth.
3. If you want, top the smoothies with extra cinnamon and toasted walnuts or pecans.
4. Serve immediately and enjoy your delicious Ninja Apple Cinnamon Smoothie!

3. ALMOND CHERRY SMOOTHIE

The Almond Cherry Smoothie is a delicious and healthy beverage that's perfect for those looking for a nutrient-packed and dairy-free option. The smoothie includes ingredients such as frozen cherries, spinach, almond butter, and almond milk, which are all rich in vitamins and antioxidants. The optional protein powder and cocoa or cacao powder can add additional health benefits.

This smoothie can be enjoyed at any time of the day, whether it's for breakfast, a mid-day snack, or even as a post-workout recovery drink. This beverage is particularly beneficial for those who seek to incorporate more fruits and vegetables into their meals or have lactose intolerance or dairy allergies.

Prep Time: 5 Mins

Cook Time: 5 Mins

Total Time: 10 Mins

Servings: 1

Ingredients

- 1 ripe banana, preferably frozen
- 1/4 tspof almond extract
- 1/2 cup of almond milk (or your preferred dairy-free milk)
- 1 tspof vanilla extract
- 1 tbsp of almond butter
- Optional add-ins: 1 scoop of your favorite protein powder and/or 1 tbsp of cocoa or cacao powder
- 2 cups of organic spinach
- 1 cup of frozen cherries (or a mix of cherries and berries)

Instructions

152 Gather all the ingredients and add them to a high-powered blender.
252 Blend the ingredients until the mixture is smooth and creamy.
352 If needed, pour additional milk to attain the consistency that you desire.
452 Transfer the smoothie into a glass and serve promptly.
552 If you wish to prepare more than one serving, you may double the recipe as desired. Enjoy your smoothie!

4. APPLE PIE SMOOTHIE

Apple Pie Smoothie is a delicious and healthy beverage made with fresh apples, milk, Greek yogurt, and a blend of apple pie spice or cinnamon. It is sweetened with maple syrup or honey and can be topped with whipped cream, apple slices, cinnamon sticks, or ground cinnamon for added flavor.

This smoothie is perfect for those who want to enjoy the flavors of apple pie in a healthier and more convenient way. It is a great source of fiber, vitamins, and minerals that can aid in digestion, boost immunity, and provide energy throughout the day.

It can be enjoyed as a breakfast smoothie, midday snack, or post-workout beverage. You can consumed it any time of the year, but it is especially enjoyable during the fall season when apples are in season.

Prep Time: 5 Mins | Cook Time: 0 Mins

Total Time: 5 Mins | Servings: 2

Ingredients

- 2 apples, cored and chopped
- 1 ½ cups of unsweetened milk of choice
- ½ cup of vanilla Greek yogurt, or plain
- 1 tspapple pie spice or cinnamon
- 1 tspmaple syrup or honey to taste, optional to sweeten
- ½ cup of ice cubes

Optional toppings

- Whipped cream
- Apple slices
- Cinnamon sticks
- Ground cinnamon

Instructions

1. Begin by coring and chopping 2 apples and placing them in a high-speed blender.
2. Add 1 ½ cups of your preferred unsweetened milk and ½ cup of vanilla Greek yogurt (or plain).
3. Next, add 1 tspof apple pie spice or cinnamon, and 1 tspof maple syrup or honey (optional) to sweeten the smoothie.
4. Add ½ cup of ice cubes to the blender.
5. Blend all the ingredients in blender until the mixture is smooth.
6. Taste the mixture and add more maple syrup or honey if you prefer a sweeter smoothie.
7. If you prefer a thicker smoothie, add more ice cubes and blend again.
8. Pour the smoothie into a glass or jar.
9. For an extra touch, you can add whipped cream, apple slices, cinnamon sticks, or ground cinnamon as toppings.
10. Serve and enjoy your delicious and healthy Apple Pie Smoothie!

5.BNANA NUTELLA MILKSHAKE

Banana Nutella Milkshake is a delicious and creamy beverage that combines the sweet and nutty flavors of Nutella with the natural sweetness of bananas. While it is a tasty treat, it is important to note that this milkshake is not the healthiest option due to its high sugar and calorie content.

It is recommended to consume this milkshake as an occasional indulgence rather than a regular part of one's diet. Additionally, those who are lactose intolerant or have a nut allergy should avoid this recipe or make modifications to suit their dietary needs.

Banana Nutella Milkshake is perfect for those who enjoy sweet and indulgent desserts or are looking for a fun and creative way to incorporate more fruits into their diet. It can be enjoyed as a refreshing beverage during hot weather or as a dessert after a meal.

Prep Time: 5 Mins

Cook Time: 0 Mins

Total Time: 5 Mins

Servings: 2

Ingredients:

- 1 ripe banana
- 2 tbsp of Nutella
- 1 cup of milk
- 1 tspof vanilla extract (optional)
- 1 cup of ice, or more if you prefer

Instructions:

1. First, peel the ripe banana and break it into small pieces.
2. Add the banana pieces, Nutella, milk, vanilla extract (if using) and ice into a blender.
3. Blend all ingredients until they are smooth and well combined.
4. If your milkshake is too thick, add more milk or ice until it reaches your desired consistency.
5. Pour the banana Nutella milkshake into glasses.
6. Serve the milkshake immediately and enjoy its delicious flavor and creamy texture.

6. BANANA OATMEAL SMOOTHIE

The Banana Oatmeal Smoothie is a healthy and tasty drink prepared with rolled oats, frozen banana, almond milk, and ground cinnamon. This smoothie is ideal for anyone seeking for a nutritious and filling breakfast or snack.

The rolled oats in the smoothie provide fiber, which can help you feel fuller and satiated for longer. The frozen banana adds natural sweetness and potassium, which is necessary for good blood pressure and heart function. Almond milk is a non-dairy substitute that is abundant in vitamin E and low in calories.

This smoothie is an excellent choice for those seeking to increase their intake of whole grains and plant-based foods. It is also an option for those who are lactose intolerant or averse to dairy.

This smoothie is best consumed in the morning as a meal or as a mid-morning snack. It can give you a quick boost of energy and help you remain focused throughout the day. It can, however, be consumed as a healthy and delicious drink at any time of day.

Prep Time: 10 Mins

Cook Time: 0 Mins

Total Time: 10 Mins

Servings: 1

Ingredients:

- 1/2 cup of (45g) rolled oats
- 1 cup of (240ml) almond milk
- 1 large banana, sliced and frozen
- 1/2 tspground cinnamon
-

Instructions:

1. Add the rolled oats to a blender and pulse until they resemble fine crumbs.
2. Add the sliced and frozen banana, almond milk, and ground cinnamon to the blender.
3. Blend the ingredients until completely smooth and combined. If the smoothie is too thick for your liking, add more milk and blend again.
4. Pour the smoothie into a glass.
5. Serve and enjoy your delicious and healthy Banana Oatmeal Smoothie!

7. BANANA CHOCOLATE SMOOTHIE

This smoothie is a great source of nutrients such as fiber, protein, and healthy fats from almond butter and chia seeds. Furthermore, it serves as a notable source of potassium, which is vital for sustaining healthy blood pressure and heart activity.

It's best to consume this smoothie in the morning or as a post-workout snack to refuel your body. However, it can be enjoyed at any time of the day.

This smoothie is perfect for anyone who wants to increase their nutrient intake or is looking for a healthy snack or meal replacement option. It is also a great option for individuals who follow a vegan or dairy-free diet.

Prep Time: 5 Mins

Cook Time: 0 Mins

Total Time: 5 Mins

Servings: 4

Ingredients:

- 1 tbsp chia seeds
- 1 1/2 tbsp unsweetened cocoa powder
- 1/2 cup of ice
- 2 medium bananas, peeled, sliced, and frozen
- 1 cup of Silk Unsweetened Vanilla Almond Milk
- 2 tbsp almond butter

Instructions:

1. Reserve 4 banana slices for garnishing the prepared smoothie. Place the remaining banana slices, almond butter, Silk Unsweetened Vanilla Almond Milk, chia seeds, cocoa powder, and ice in a blender jar.
2. Puree the ingredients on high speed or on the "smoothie" setting (if available) until completely smooth.
3. Divide the mixture between four cups or glasses.
4. If desired, garnish the top of each cup of with mini chocolate chips, sliced almonds, and the reserved banana slices for a nice presentation.
5. Serve the Banana Chocolate Smoothie immediately with a spoon.

8. BANANA SPLIT SMOOTHIE

The Banana Split Smoothie is a healthy and delicious beverage that is perfect for breakfast, snack, or dessert. This smoothie is made with frozen bananas, cacao powder, almond butter, almond milk, and vanilla extract, which provides a good source of fiber, potassium, antioxidants, and healthy fats. It is also naturally sweetened with dates, making it a great alternative to sugar-loaded drinks.

For individuals who crave something sweet but do not want to compromise their health, this smoothie is the perfect blend of nutritious and delicious. It is also perfect for those who are on a plant-based or vegan diet.

It is recommended to drink this smoothie in the morning or as a pre or post-workout drink, as it provides a good source of energy and helps with muscle recovery. It can also be enjoyed as a refreshing and healthy dessert.

Prep Time: 10 Mins | Cook Time: 0 Mins

Total Time: 10 Mins | Servings: 2

Ingredients:

Smoothie:

- 1/4 cup of unsweetened almond milk (more as needed for preferred thickness)
- 1/2 tspvanilla extract
- 2 medium-large ripe bananas, sliced and frozen
- 2 pitted dates (optional, for extra sweetness)
- 2 tbsp cacao powder (or cocoa powder)
- 1 tbsp salted almond butter (if unsalted, add a pinch of sea salt)

Toppings:

- Ripe cherries
- 1 just-ripe banana, peeled and sliced lengthwise
- Coconut whipped cream
- 1 tbsp cacao nibs
- 1 tbsp shredded unsweetened coconut

Instructions:

1. Add the frozen banana slices, cacao powder, almond butter, and almond milk to a blender. Blend on low speed until the mixture reaches a thick and creamy consistency, pausing occasionally to scrape down the sides of the blender. The texture should resemble that of soft-serve ice cream.
2. Add the vanilla extract and pitted dates (if using) to the blender. Blend again until the mixture is well blended, thick, and creamy. Taste and adjust the flavor as needed by adding more almond butter, vanilla extract, salt, or cacao powder.

3. While preparing the serving glasses, set the blender with the smoothie in the freezer or refrigerator.
4. Cut a banana in half lengthwise and peel. Then slice in half lengthwise again to get four pieces. Slide the banana wedges down into two serving glasses (or one large serving glass) and press them with a spoon to adhere to the sides.
5. Pour the smoothie mixture into the serving glasses and top with desired toppings such as coconut whipped cream, ripe cherries, shredded coconut, and cacao nibs.
6. Best when fresh but can be covered and frozen for up to 2 days. Before enjoying, let the smoothie thaw if it has been frozen.

09. BLACKBERRY BANANA SMOOTHIE

The Blackberry Banana Smoothie is a healthy and refreshing beverage that combines the sweetness of bananas with the tartness of blackberries. This smoothie is a great source of vitamins, minerals, and antioxidants, which can help boost your immune system and protect your body against disease.

The Greek yogurt in this recipe provides protein and probiotics, which are good for gut health. The honey is a natural sweetener and contains antioxidants and antibacterial properties.

To feel full and energized, it is best to enjoy this smoothie as a breakfast option in the morning or as a midday snack. It's a great option for people who are looking for a healthy and nutritious alternative to sugary drinks or snacks.

Prep Time: 5 Mins

Cook Time: 0 Mins

Total Time: 5 Mins

Servings: 2

Ingredients:

- 1 peeled banana
- 1 cup of chilled blackberries (130g)
- ½ cup of Greek yogurt (130g)
- 2 tsp of honey

Instructions:

1. Add the blackberries, banana, yogurt, and honey into a blender.
2. Blend the ingredients together until they become smooth.
3. Once the mixture has blended together, remove it from the blender.
4. Serve the smoothie immediately.

10. BLACK FOREST SMOOTHIE

Drinking black forest smoothie can help boost energy, promote weight loss, improve digestion, and support overall health and wellness. It is also a great alternative to sugary and processed drinks, as it is low in calories and high in nutrients.

The best time to drink black forest smoothie is in the morning or after a workout, as it can help replenish your body with essential nutrients and promote muscle recovery. However, you can enjoy it any time of the day as a healthy snack or meal replacement.

Whether you're an athlete, fitness enthusiast, busy professional, or simply aiming to increase your fruit and vegetable intake, this smoothie is an excellent option for boosting your health and wellbeing.

Prep Time: 5 Mins

Cook Time: 0 Mins

Total Time: 5 Mins

Servings: 1

Ingredients:

- 1 cup of unsweetened almond milk (240 ml)
- 1 tbsp of chia seeds (7 g)
- 2 tbsp of unsweetened cocoa powder
- 1 scoop (30 g) of your favorite protein powder (optional)
- 1/4 cup of rolled oats (20 g)*
- 1 cup of frozen cherries
- 1-2 handfuls of baby spinach (optional)
- 1-2 Medjool dates (15-30 g), depending on desired sweetness

Instructions

1. Add all the ingredients into a standard blender.
2. Blend the mixture until smooth.
3. If you prefer a thicker and creamier smoothie, you can make it in advance and store it in the fridge.
4. Transfer the smoothie into a glass and savor it!

11. BLUEBERRY ACAI SMOOTHIE

The Blueberry Acai Smoothie is a delicious and nutritious beverage that combines the antioxidant-rich properties of blueberries and acai powder. This vibrant, purple smoothie is packed with antioxidants, minerals, and vitamins making it an excellent choice for individuals seeking to boost their immune system and maintain overall health.

Ideal for consumption at any time of the day, this smoothie is particularly beneficial as a refreshing morning pick-me-up or a post-workout recovery drink. Thanks to its low calorie content and abundance of nutrients, it is perfect for health-conscious individuals, athletes, or those looking for a tasty way to incorporate more fruits into their diet.

In addition, the Blueberry Acai Smoothie is a fantastic option for people who are lactose intolerant or prefer plant-based alternatives, as it uses almond milk or any other plant milk of choice. Whether you're aiming for a healthier lifestyle or just craving a delicious treat, this smoothie is a perfect choice.

Prep Time:10 Minutes

Total Time: 10 Minutes

Serving: 1

Ingredients

- 1 sliced and frozen banana
- 1 cup of fresh or frozen blueberries
- 2 tbsp acai powder
- 1/2 cup of almond milk (or any plant milk of your choice)

Tools

- Blender

Instructions

1. Gather all the ingredients - a sliced and frozen banana, blueberries (fresh or frozen), acai powder, and almond milk (or any plant milk of your choice).
2. Place all the ingredients into the blender.
3. Blend the ingredients until a smooth consistency is achieved.
4. Pour the smoothie mixture into glasses.
5. Savor and enjoy your perfectly crafted Blueberry Acai Smoothie.

12. BLUEBERRY BANANA SMOOTHIE

The Blueberry Banana Smoothie is a delightful and nutritious beverage that combines the natural sweetness of blueberries and bananas with the creaminess of oat milk. This smoothie is an excellent source of vitamins, minerals, and antioxidants, making it perfect for individuals who want to maintain a healthy diet or who are looking for a quick energy boost.

The added hemp seeds and oats provide protein and fiber, while the Ceylon cinnamon brings a subtle warmth to the flavor profile. The versatility of this smoothie makes it an ideal choice for those with specific dietary requirements or preferences, as it can be easily adapted to suit different tastes and needs.

This refreshing and nourishing smoothie is perfect for breakfast or afternoon snack, providing you with sustained energy throughout the day. It is particularly well-suited for active individuals, busy professionals, and health-conscious individuals who want a delicious and simple method to incorporate more fruits and nutrients into their daily routine.

Prep Time:5 Minutes | Total Time: 5 Minutes

Serving: 1

Ingredients

- 1/2 cup of fresh or frozen blueberries
- 1/2 banana
- 1 cup of oat milk
- 1 tbsp hemp seeds
- 2 tbsp oats
- 1 tspCeylon cinnamon
- A handful of ice cubes (optional)
- Sweetener of choice (optional): Maple syrup, honey, or dates, to taste
- Toppings: dark chocolate, cacao nibs, hemp seeds

Instructions

1. Begin by placing all the ingredients in your blender. To ensure smooth blending, add the wet ingredients first, followed by the ice cubes if you choose to use them.
2. Blend the mixture at a high speed until it achieves a silky-smooth consistency.
3. Check if the smoothie is too thick, add a little more liquid, such as milk or water. Blend once more to properly blend.
4. Taste your smoothie and, if necessary, sweeten it further to your liking. You can use 1-2 soaked dates, date syrup, raw honey, maple syrup, stevia, or your preferred low-carb sweetener.
5. Pour the smoothie into a tall glass.
6. Add your chosen toppings; in this recipe, we used hemp seeds and cacao nibs. Feel free to get creative with your favorite toppings.
7. Serve your smoothie and savor the flavor!

13. BLUEBERRY BLAST SMOOTHIE

Blueberry Blast Smoothie is a delicious and nutritious drink made with frozen blueberries, Greek yogurt, orange juice, frozen banana, and vanilla extract. It is packed with antioxidants, fiber, and vitamins, making it a healthy drink option for people looking to boost their immunity and overall health.

The smoothie can be consumed any time of the day, preferably in the morning or as a snack between meals. It is a perfect drink for people who want to have a quick and healthy meal on the go, as well as for fitness enthusiasts who need to refuel after a workout.

However, it is essential to note that while the Blueberry Blast Smoothie is healthy, it is not a meal replacement and should be consumed as part of a balanced diet. Also, individuals with lactose intolerance should be cautious when consuming Greek yogurt, as it contains lactose.

Prep Time:5 Minutes

Total Time: 5 Minutes

Serving: 1

Ingredients

- 2 cups of frozen unsweetened blueberries (make sure not to thaw them)
- 1/2 cup of 100% orange juice (preferably calcium-fortified)
- 3/4 cup of reduced fat vanilla Greek yogurt
- 1/2 medium frozen banana
- 1/2 tsp. pure vanilla extract

Instructions

1. Get your blender and add in the frozen blueberries, orange juice, Greek yogurt, frozen banana, and pure vanilla extract.
2. Cover the blender securely and blend for 30 to 35 seconds or until the mixture becomes thick and smooth.
3. If you prefer a thinner consistency, you may add more orange juice. If you prefer a thicker smoothie, though, add extra frozen fruit.
4. Once done blending, pour the mixture into two glasses.
5. Serve the Blueberry Blast Smoothie immediately and enjoy!

14. BLUEBERRY CHEESECAKE SMOOTHIE

The Blueberry Cheesecake Smoothie is a delicious and nutritious beverage that combines the flavors of a classic cheesecake with the health benefits of blueberries and spinach. This smoothie is perfect for individuals looking for a healthier alternative to satisfy their dessert cravings while incorporating essential vitamins and antioxidants.

Rich in antioxidants, fiber, and vitamin C from blueberries, along with calcium and probiotics from Greek yogurt, this smoothie supports a strong immune system and promotes gut health. The optional spinach addition provides an extra boost of iron, calcium, and vitamins A and K.

Ideal for breakfast or a midday snack, the Blueberry Cheesecake Smoothie is suitable for health-conscious individuals, athletes, and busy professionals seeking a quick and nutritious option. This beverage is also an excellent choice for people with a sweet tooth who want to indulge without compromising their dietary goals.

Prep Time:5 Minutes

Total Time: 5 Minutes

Serving: 1

Ingredients:

- 1 cup of almond milk (or any preferred dairy or non-dairy milk)
- A few handfuls of spinach (optional)
- 1 cup of frozen blueberries
- 5.3 oz. container of vanilla or plain Greek yogurt (approximately 1/2 cup of plus 1 tablespoon); if using plain yogurt, include 1/4 tspof vanilla extract and a touch of honey or preferred sweetener, according to taste
- 2 tbsp of regular or light cream cheese
- A minuscule pinch of salt and 3 to 5 ice cubes
- Optional: crushed graham crackers for garnishing

Instructions

1. Place the ingredients in the blender container in the sequence provided.
2. Activate the blender and continue blending until a smooth texture is achieved.
3. If desired, add a sprinkle of crushed graham crackers on top for garnish.

15. BLUEBERRY GINGER GREEN SMOOTHIE

The Blueberry Ginger Green Smoothie is a healthy and nutritious drink made with ingredients such as blueberries, spinach, ginger, and almond milk. This smoothie is high in antioxidants, vitamins, and minerals, all of which assist to enhance the immune system, aid digestion, and promote general health.

It is best to consume this smoothie in the morning or as a pre-workout drink, as it provides a natural energy boost and helps keep you full for longer periods. This smoothie is perfect for people who follow a vegan, vegetarian, or gluten-free diet, as it is free of animal products and gluten.

However, individuals with allergies to any of the ingredients used in this smoothie should exercise caution and consult their healthcare provider before consuming it. Overall, the Blueberry Ginger Green Smoothie is a tasty and healthy drink that anyone trying to improve their health and well-being can enjoy.

Prep Time: 10 Minutes | Total Time: 10 Minutes

Serving: 2

Ingredients

- 1 cup of unsweetened almond milk and 1 cup of frozen blueberries
- 1 small frozen banana and 1 cup of baby spinach
- 1-inch piece of ginger, chopped (approximately 1 tbsp when chopped)
- Juice from ½ a lemon (approximately 1 tablespoon)
- Optional toppings and add-ins:
- Dash of cinnamon or turmeric
- 1-2 scoops plain or vanilla protein powder
- 1 tbsp chia, hemp, or flax seeds

Instructions:

1. Gather all the ingredients and place them in a high-powered blender.
2. Begin blending the ingredients on low speed, then gradually increase the speed to high.Blend the ingredients until they become smooth and creamy.
3. If you choose to use any of the optional toppings or add-ins, you can add them at this point and blend again until combined.
4. Pour the mixture into two glasses and sprinkle some cinnamon on top, if you desire.
5. Serve and enjoy your Blueberry Ginger Green Smoothie!

16. BLUEBERRY ORANGE SMOOTHIE

"Blueberry Orange Smoothie" is a nutritious and refreshing drink that may be consumed at any time of day. It contains frozen blueberries, orange juice, orange peel, and Greek Fat Free blueberry yogurt. The smoothie is rich in antioxidants, vitamins, and minerals that are beneficial for overall health. It's an excellent source of fiber and helps to boost the immune system. The smoothie is low in calories and perfect for those who are watching their weight. It's ideal for people who have a busy lifestyle and want a quick and healthy snack. The best time to drink the Blueberry Orange Smoothie is in the morning or as a midday snack to keep you energized throughout the day.

Prep Time:5 Minutes

Total Time: 5 Minutes

Serving: 2

Ingredients

- 1 cup of frozen blueberries
- 1/2 cup of orange juice
- 1 tspof grated orange peel
- 1 container (6 oz) of Greek Fat Free blueberry yogurt

Instructions

1. Take a high-powered blender and add all the ingredients into it.
2. Begin blending at a low speed and gradually increase the speed to high.
3. Blend the mixture until it turns creamy and smooth.
4. Take two glasses and pour the smoothie into them.
5. You may add a sprinkle of cinnamon on top as a garnish, if desired.

17. BLUEBERRY PEACH SMOOTHIE

Blueberry Peach Smoothie is a healthy and refreshing beverage that is ideal for those looking for a nutritious and delightful beverage. It is made with frozen blueberries and peaches, chia seeds or collagen protein, spinach or greens, orange juice, and water or almond milk.

This smoothie is packed with essential vitamins, minerals, and antioxidants that are beneficial for overall health. Blueberries are rich in fiber, vitamin C, and vitamin K, while peaches are a good source of vitamin A and potassium. The chia seeds or collagen protein provide added protein and help to promote healthy skin, hair, and nails.

The smoothie is best consumed in the morning or as a midday snack to provide a quick energy boost. It is a good choice for individuals who are looking to increase their fruit and vegetable intake or for those who want to incorporate a healthy drink into their daily routine.

Overall, the Blueberry Peach Smoothie is a delicious and nutritious drink that can help to promote overall health and wellness.

Prep Time:5 Minutes | Total Time: 5 Minutes

Serving: 2

Ingredients

- 1 1/2 cups of frozen blueberries
- 1 1/2 cups of frozen peaches
- 2 tbsp chia seeds or 2 scoops collagen protein
- 1 cup of spinach or greens (optional)
- 1 cup of orange juice
- 1/2–1 cup of water or almond milk

Instructions:

1. Prepare all the ingredients by measuring them out and having them ready to use.
2. Put the frozen blueberries and peaches into the blender.
3. If using chia seeds or collagen protein, sprinkle them on top of the fruit.
4. If using greens, add them to the blender as well.
5. Pour the orange juice and water or almond milk over the ingredients.
6. Cover the blender and blend on high speed until completely smooth.
7. Check the consistency of the smoothie and add more juice or water as needed to reach the desired thickness.
8. Blend again until it gets smooth.
9. Pour the smoothie into glasses and serve right away.

18. BLUEBERRY POMEGRANATE SMOOTHIE

Blueberry Pomegranate Smoothie is a healthy and refreshing drink made with frozen blueberries, chilled pomegranate juice, honey, and vanilla fat-free yogurt. It is a great post-workout drink as it provides a combination of protein and honey that helps muscles recover after exercise. This smoothie is ideal for health-conscious individuals who want to boost their immunity and maintain their overall well-being. It can be consumed at any time of the day, but it is especially beneficial when consumed after a workout.

Prep Time:5 Minutes

Total Time: 5 Minutes

Serving: 2

Ingredients

- 2 cups of frozen blueberries
- 1 cup of chilled 100% pomegranate juice
- 1 tbsp of honey
- 1 (6-ounce) carton of vanilla fat-free yogurt

Instructions

1. Get a blender and put all of the above ingredients in it.
2. Mix the ingredients together until the mixture is smooth.
3. Pour the smoothie right away into a glass and serve.

19. BLUEBERRY SPINACH SMOOTHIE

The Blueberry Spinach Smoothie is a healthy and tasty drink that you can drink any time on a day. Packed with nutrients and antioxidants, this smoothie is perfect for anyone looking to improve their overall health and well-being. The combination of spinach and blueberries provides a variety of vitamins and minerals, while the Greek yogurt adds protein and a creamy texture. This smoothie is also a great option for those with dietary restrictions, as it can easily be made dairy-free using coconut yogurt.

It is recommended to drink the Blueberry Spinach Smoothie in the morning as a breakfast option, or as a midday snack to help boost energy levels. It is also a great post-workout drink, as the protein and nutrients can help aid in muscle recovery.

Overall, the Blueberry Spinach Smoothie is a delicious and nutritious drink that is perfect for anyone looking to improve their health and add more fruits and vegetables to their diet.

Prep Time:5 Minutes

Total Time: 5 Minutes

Serving: 3

Ingredients

- 1 cup of loosely packed spinach
- 1 cup of milk of your choice (or more, to taste)
- 1/2 cup of plain Greek yogurt (or coconut yogurt for a dairy-free option)
- 2 cups of frozen blueberries (if using fresh, add ice to the smoothie)
- 1 ripe banana
- a dash of cinnamon (optional)

Instructions

1. In your blender, combine the spinach, milk, and yogurt. Blend until the mixture is smooth and there are no bits of spinach left.
2. Add the frozen blueberries, banana, and cinnamon (if using) to the blender. Blend again until everything is well combined.
3. Taste the smoothie and make any necessary changes to the consistency. If you want the consistency to be thinner, you can add more milk or water.
4. Pour the smoothie into a T-shaped glass and enjoy it immediately.

20. CARAMEL APPLE SMOOTHIE

Caramel Apple Smoothie is a tasty and nutritious beverage made with nonfat or almond milk, unsweetened apple juice, fresh apple chunks, sugar-free caramel syrup, and ice cubes. This smoothie is an excellent source of fiber, vitamins, and antioxidants, making it a healthy drink option. It is perfect for people who are looking for a quick and easy breakfast. However, the high sugar content in caramel syrup should be noted, making it less suitable for those who are watching their sugar intake. This smoothie can be enjoyed at any time of the day, but it is best consumed as a meal replacement during breakfast or after a workout for a quick energy boost.

Prep Time: 10 Minutes

Total Time: 10 Minutes

Serving: 1

Ingredients

- 3/4 cup of milk (nonfat or almond milk can be used as a substitute)
- 1/4 cup of unsweetened apple juice
- 1 apple (use your preferred brand)
- 1 tbsp of sugar-free caramel syrup (plus extra for garnishing, if desired)
- 2 cups of ice cubes

Instructions

1. Pour the milk and apple juice into a blender.
2. Core the apple and cut it into chunks. Add it to the blender along with the caramel syrup and ice.
3. Blend the ingredients until smooth.
4. If desired, top the smoothie with additional caramel syrup before serving.

21. CINNAMON ROLL SMOOTHIE

The "Cinnamon Roll Smoothie" is a tasty and healthy drink that is perfect for people who want a quick and easy breakfast or snack. Made with vanilla almond milk, vanilla Greek yogurt, old-fashioned oats, brown sugar, cinnamon, and a frozen banana, this smoothie is a great source of protein, fiber, and antioxidants.

Due to its high sugar content from the brown sugar and banana, it is recommended to drink this smoothie in moderation as part of a balanced diet. It is perfect for people who are looking for a healthy alternative to traditional cinnamon rolls but still want to enjoy the delicious taste of cinnamon. This smoothie is also suitable for vegetarians and can be customized to meet different dietary needs by substituting ingredients as necessary. It is best served immediately after blending to ensure optimal taste and texture.

Prep Time: 2 Minutes

Cook Time: 2 Minutes

Total Time: 4 Minutes

Serving: 2

Ingredients

- 1 cup of vanilla almond milk
- 1/2 cup of vanilla Greek yogurt
- 1/4 cup of old-fashioned oats
- 1 tbsp of brown sugar
- 1/4 tspof cinnamon
- 1 frozen banana

Instructions

1. Add all the ingredients into a blender.
2. Mix the ingredients together until they are smooth and mixed well.
3. If you want the consistency to be thicker, you can add more oats or banana. If you want the consistency to be thinner, add more almond milk.
4. Taste the smoothie and adjust the sweetness and cinnamon to your liking.
5. Pour the smoothie right away into a glass and serve

22. CARROT CAKE SMOOTHIE

The Carrot Cake Smoothie is a delightful and nutritious beverage that combines the flavors of a classic carrot cake with the health benefits of fresh ingredients. Packed with vitamins, minerals, and antioxidants from raw carrots, pineapple, and banana, this smoothie offers a boost to your immune system and overall well-being. The addition of Greek yogurt and gluten-free oats provides a dose of protein and fiber, making it a satisfying and energizing drink.

Ideal for those with gluten sensitivities or those seeking a healthy alternative to traditional desserts, this smoothie is perfect for any time of the day. It can be enjoyed as a refreshing morning treat, a satisfying post-workout replenishment, or an evening pick-me-up. The Carrot Cake Smoothie is a fantastic choice for health-conscious individuals, busy professionals, or anyone looking for a delicious and nourishing drink that supports a well-balanced diet.

Prep Time: 5 Minutes

Total Time: 5 Minutes

Serving: 1

Ingredients

- 1 sizable raw carrot, chopped (or grated if not using a high-performance blender like Vitamix)
- 1 medium frozen ripe banana
- 1/2 cup of frozen pineapple pieces
- 3/4 cup of light coconut milk (or any preferred milk), add more if needed
- 1/4 cup of unflavored Greek yogurt
- 1/4 cup of gluten-free oats
- 1 tbsp pecan butter or almond butter
- 1 tsp vanilla essence
- 1/2 tsp powdered cinnamon
- A dash of nutmeg

Instructions

1. Place all the ingredients into a large, high-powered blender.
2. Blend at a high speed for 1-2 minutes or until the mixture is smooth and all the ingredients are thoroughly combined.
3. If required, add more milk to achieve the desired smoothie consistency.

23. CARROT GINGER SMOOTHIE

Carrot Ginger Smoothie is a delicious and healthy beverage that is perfect for those who are health-conscious and looking for a refreshing drink. This smoothie is made with chopped carrots, ginger, yogurt, coconut milk, honey, and ice.

Carrots have a lot of vitamin A, and ginger is known for being good at reducing inflammation. Coconut milk provides healthy fats and adds creaminess to the smoothie. Yogurt provides probiotics, which promote digestive health.

This smoothie is ideal for drinking in the morning or as a post-workout beverage. It can be a perfect addition to a healthy breakfast or a nutritious snack throughout the day.

Overall, the Carrot Ginger Smoothie is a great choice for anyone who wants a healthy drink that tastes great and is full of vitamins, nutrients, and other good things for your body.

Prep Time: 5 Minutes

Total Time: 5 Minutes

Serving: 2

Ingredients

- 3 cups of chopped carrots (with peel on)
- 1-inch piece of ginger, peeled and chopped into smaller chunks
- 1/3 cup of plain yogurt (coconut milk yogurt can be used)
- 1 cup of full-fat canned coconut milk* (full-fat is recommended)
- 1 tbsp of honey (adjust to taste)
- 1/2 cup of ice

Instructions:

1. Add all the ingredients into a blender.
2. Blend until the mixture becomes smooth and there are no chunks remaining.
3. If needed, add more coconut milk or almond milk to help process the smoothie.
4. Pour into a glass and enjoy your refreshing Carrot Ginger Smoothie!

24. CHERRY BERRY SMOOTHIE

Cherry Berry Smoothie is a tasty and healthy drink that can be made quickly and is great for breakfast or a snack. This smoothie is a great source of vitamins, minerals, and antioxidants. It is made with fresh or frozen unsweetened pitted red tart cherries, low-fat milk, plain fat-free or low-fat yogurt, fresh or frozen unsweetened blueberries or raspberries, frozen tart cherry juice or cranberry juice concentrate, honey, vanilla, and ice cubes.

Smoothies can be consumed at any time of day, but they are especially good in the morning because they give you energy to start the day. It is also an excellent post-workout drink, as it can help replenish lost nutrients and aid in muscle recovery.

Cherry Berry Smoothie is perfect for individuals who are looking for a low-calorie and low-fat drink option, as it contains no added sugar and is low in fat. It's also a good choice for people who want to eat more fruits and vegetables because it has a variety of fruits and gives you more than one serving of fruit in each smoothie.

Prep Time: 10 Minutes

Total Time: 10 Minutes

Serving: 2

Ingredients

- ½ cup of fresh or frozen unsweetened pitted red tart cherries
- ½ cup of low-fat milk and 8 ice cubes
- ¼ cup of plain fat-free or low-fat yogurt
- 2 tbsp fresh or frozen unsweetened blueberries or raspberries
- 1 tbsp frozen tart cherry juice or cranberry juice concentrate, thawed
- 1 tbsp honey and ½ tspvanilla

Instructions

1. In a blender, combine 1/2 cup of cherries, milk, yogurt, blueberries, juice concentrate, honey, and vanilla.
2. Cover the blender and blend for about 45 seconds or until the mixture is smooth.
3. Add the ice cubes to the blender.
4. Cover the blender again and blend for an additional 15 seconds or until the mixture is smooth then Pour the smoothie into two chilled glasses.
5. Optionally, you can top each glass with additional cherries or chopped dried cherries. Also This recipe makes 2 servings.

25. CHERRY VANILLA ALMOND SMOOTHIE

Cherry Vanilla Almond Smoothie is a healthy and delicious drink that is packed with nutrients, making it a perfect option for people who are health-conscious. It contains ingredients like spinach, almond milk, chia seeds, and frozen cherries, which are rich in vitamins, minerals, and antioxidants that promote good health.

The smoothie is an excellent source of protein, calcium, and fiber, which can help keep you feeling full for longer and promote healthy digestion. Also, it has few calories, which makes it a good drink for people who are trying to lose weight or keep their weight at a healthy level.

The smoothie can be consumed at any time of the day, but it is especially beneficial when consumed in the morning as a healthy breakfast alternative. It provides a fast and easy way to get all the essential nutrients that your body needs to start the day.

Overall, the Cherry Vanilla Almond Smoothie is perfect for anyone who wants to live a healthy life without giving up taste. It is an excellent option for people who are lactose intolerant or allergic to dairy, as it is made with almond milk instead of cow's milk.

Prep Time: 5 Minutes

Total Time: 5 Minutes

Serving: 1

Ingredients

- 1/2 cup of baby spinach and 1 cup of frozen cherries
- 1 cup of unsweetened almond milk
- 1/2 cup of cottage cheese or plain Greek yogurt
- 1 tspchia seeds and/or 1 scoop protein powder or collagen powder
- 1 tspalmond butter and 1 tspvanilla extract
- 3-5 ice cubes (depending on the desired texture)
- Honey, sugar, stevia or any sweetener of your choice (if needed) to taste

Instructions

1. Begin by placing all the ingredients into your blender in the same order listed above.
2. Next, select the smoothie cycle or pulse a few times then slowly increase the speed until you reach the maximum speed.
3. Stop blending once the desired texture is achieved.Pour the smoothie into glasses and enjoy!

26. CHERRY VANILLA SMOOTHIE

Cherry Vanilla Smoothie is a delicious and healthy beverage that is perfect for breakfast or a refreshing snack. This smoothie, prepared with frozen sweet cherries, vanilla yogurt, vanilla essence, milk, and citrus zest, is high in antioxidants, vitamins, and minerals that promote good health.

Cherry Vanilla Smoothie is a great choice for people looking for a quick and easy way to add more fruit to their diet. It is also a good option for those with a sweet tooth, as the natural sweetness of the cherries and vanilla yogurt make it a satisfying treat.

This smoothie can be consumed at any time of day, but it is particularly beneficial when consumed as a breakfast beverage in the morning. It provides the body with essential nutrients and energy to kickstart the day.

Overall, Cherry Vanilla Smoothie is a healthy and tasty option for anyone looking to add more fruits and dairy to their diet. It is ideal for people who are health-conscious or wanting to lose weight because it is high in nutrients and low in calories

Prep Time: 5 Minutes

Total Time: 5 Minutes

Serving: 1

Ingredients

- 1 1/2 cups of frozen sweet cherries
- 1/2 cup of vanilla yogurt
- 1/4 tspof vanilla extract
- 1 cup of milk
- Zest of one orange

Instructions

1. Begin by adding all of the ingredients into a blender.
2. Mix the ingredients together until they are smooth and mixed well.
3. If desired, top the smoothie with some additional frozen cherries.
4. Pour the smoothie into glasses and enjoy!

27. CHOCOLATE ALMOND SMOOTHIE

Chocolate Almond Smoothie is a healthy and delicious beverage that is perfect for people looking for a quick and nutritious snack or breakfast option. It contains unsweetened oat milk, banana, rolled oats, almond butter, cocoa powder, and crushed ice, all of which are nutritious ingredients that provide energy and nourishment to the body.

This smoothie is high in fiber, protein, and healthy fats, making it great for those who wish to live a healthy lifestyle. It also helps to keep you full and content for extended periods of time, which can help with weight loss.

Because of its rich fiber and nutritional content, it is best to consume this smoothie in the morning as a breakfast replacement or as a mid-day snack to keep your energy levels up.

Overall, the Chocolate Almond Smoothie is a great beverage for anyone looking for a healthy and tasty option that provides numerous health benefits.

Prep Time: 2 Minutes

Total Time: 2 Minutes

Serving: 1

Ingredients

- ¾ cup of unsweetened oat milk (180 mL)
- 1 sliced banana
- ⅓ cup of rolled oats (25 g)
- 2 tbsp of almond butter
- 1 tspof cocoa powder
- 1 cup of crushed ice (140 g)

Instructions

1. In a blender, add the oat milk, sliced banana, rolled oats, almond butter, cocoa powder, and crushed ice.
2. Mix the ingredients until they form a smooth paste.
3. Serve the smoothie directly in a glass.

28. CHOCOLATE AVOCADO SMOOTHIE

Chocolate Avocado Smoothie is a healthy and nutritious beverage that is perfect for people looking for a tasty and filling snack or breakfast option. It contains almond milk, ripe avocado, dates, cocoa powder, ice cubes, vanilla extract, and sliced banana, all of which are healthy ingredients that provide energy and nourishment to the body.

This smoothie is high in fiber, healthy fats, and antioxidants, making it great for those who desire to live a healthy lifestyle. The avocado has beneficial fats that help reduce inflammation and enhance heart health, while the cocoa powder contains antioxidants that can lower the risk of chronic diseases.

Overall, the Chocolate Avocado Smoothie is a great beverage for anyone looking for a healthy and tasty option that provides numerous health benefits. It is also a great option for vegans and people with dietary restrictions, as it can be easily customized to fit different dietary needs.

Prep Time: 10 Minutes

Total Time: 10 Minutes

Serving: 2

Ingredients

- 1 cup of almond milk
- 1/2 large ripe avocado with no black spots
- 4-6 soft pitted dates (or 2 tbsp of maple syrup or coconut sugar)
- 2 1/2 tbsp of unsweetened cocoa powder
- 1 cup of ice cubes and 1 small sliced banana
- 1 tspof vanilla extract
- Optional add-ons to boost your smoothie:
- 1 tbsp of unsalted peanut butter
- 1 scoop of vegan protein powde

Instructions

1. Make sure your avocado is ripe with smooth green flesh and has no black spots.
2. In a blender, add all the ingredients together, starting with 4 dates.
3. Blend the ingredients at high speed until the mixture becomes frothy and thick.
4. Taste the smoothie and adjust the number of dates, adding up to 2 Medjool dates to boost the sweetness. Serve immediately and enjoy your Chocolate Avocado Smoothie. with unsweetened coconut whipped cream melted chocolate.

29. CHOCOLATE PEANUT BUTTER BANANA SMOOTHIE

Chocolate Peanut Butter Banana Smoothie is a delicious and healthy beverage that combines the flavors of chocolate, peanut butter, and banana. It is packed with nutrients like potassium, fiber, and protein, making it a great meal replacement or snack option for people who are health-conscious.

This smoothie is perfect for those who have busy schedules and are always on-the-go, as it can be prepared quickly and easily. It can be consumed at any time of the day, whether as a breakfast, pre-workout or post-workout snack, or as a dessert.

However, because of the presence of peanut butter, this smoothie is high in calories and fat and should be eaten in moderation. It may not be suitable for individuals with peanut allergies or those who are on a low-fat diet. Overall, this smoothie is a delicious and nutritious option for those looking to incorporate more fruits and healthy fats into their diet.

Prep Time: 5 Minutes

Total Time: 5 Minutes

Serving: 1

Ingredients

- 1 ripe banana, frozen
- 1-2 tbsp cacao powder (or unsweetened cocoa powder)
- 2 tbsp natural peanut butter, creamy
- 1 tspvanilla extract
- ½ cup of unsweetened almond milk, plus more for thinning

Instructions

1. In a large, high-powered blender, combine all of the components.
2. Blend for 2 minutes on high, or until all components are thoroughly combined.
3. Begin with 1 tbsp of cacao powder, adding more as desired for a richer chocolate flavor.
4. If necessary, thin the smoothie with additional almond milk.
5. This recipe yields 1 smoothie, but feel free to double the ingredients to serve 2.

30. CHOCOLATE CHERRY ALMOND SMOOTHIE

The Chocolate Cherry Almond Smoothie is a delicious and healthy beverage that is perfect for people who are looking for a nutritious and easy-to-make drink. Made with frozen cherries, cacao or cocoa powder, natural almond butter, and non-dairy milk, this smoothie is packed with antioxidants, fiber, and healthy fats.

This smoothie is ideal for people who want to maintain a healthy weight, improve their digestive health, and boost their immune system. The smoothie is also a good source of protein, making it a great post-workout drink.

This smoothie can be consumed at any time of day, whether in the morning as a breakfast drink or in the afternoon as a refreshment. It's best served cold and can be kept in the fridge for a few hours.

Overall, the Chocolate Cherry Almond Smoothie is a nutritious and tasty drink that can help improve your overall health and well-being.

Prep Time: 5 Minutes

Total Time: 5 Minutes

Serving: 1

Ingredients

- 1 cup of (140 g) of pitted frozen cherries
- 1/2 to 1 cup of (118-235 ml) of non-dairy milk (store-bought or homemade)
- 1 tbsp of cacao or cocoa powder
- 1 tbsp of natural almond butter
- 1/2 tspof almond extract
- Optional: sweetener of your choice (refer to notes)
- Other optional add-ins: 1 scoop of protein powder, 1/2 tspof cinnamon, and/or 1/2 inch piece of fresh ginger

Instructions

1. Place all the ingredients in a blender.
2. For a thicker smoothie, use less milk; for a thinner smoothie, use more milk.
3. Blend the mixture on high for 30 to 60 seconds until it becomes smooth and creamy.
4. Pour the smoothie into a drinking glass.Serve the smoothie chilled and enjoy!

31. CHOCOLATE CHERRY SMOOTHIE

Chocolate Cherry Smoothie is an excellent choice for those looking for a healthy and tasty breakfast or snack. The smoothie contains antioxidants, fiber, and protein, all of which have been shown to improve digestion, reduce inflammation, and support muscle development and repair.

The Chocolate Cherry Smoothie is best consumed in the morning or as a post-workout recovery treat. It is also appropriate for vegans, gluten-free, and dairy-free eaters.

Prep Time: 5 Minutes

Total Time: 5 Minutes

Serving: 2

Ingredients

- 1 cup of coconut milk, unsweetened (plain or vanilla)
- Optional: 1 scoop protein powder (plain or vanilla) or 2 tbsp almond butter
- Optional: 1 small medjool date (pitted and diced) or 1 tsppure maple syrup
- 2 tbsp chocolate powder, unsweetened (cocoa powder is ok too)
- 2 cups of frozen cherries

Optional toppings

- cacao nibs
- granola
- hemp hearts

Instructions

1. In a blender, add the frozen cherries, unsweetened almond milk, raw cacao powder, and the optional Medjool date or pure maple syrup.
2. If desired, add the optional protein powder or almond butter to the blender.
3. Blend the ingredients until smooth, adding a little extra almond milk as needed to achieve your desired consistency.
4. Pour the smoothie into a glass and top with your desired optional toppings, such as granola, cacao nibs, or hemp hearts.
5. Enjoy your delicious and healthy Chocolate Cherry Smoothie either by sipping it with a straw or eating it with a spoon.

32. CHOCOLATE COVERED STRAWBERRY SMOOTHIE

The Chocolate Covered Strawberry Smoothie is a healthy and delicious drink prepared with fresh or frozen strawberries, banana, protein powder, and almond milk. It is high in fiber, antioxidants, and protein, making it ideal for anyone seeking for a nutritious and filling drink. This smoothie can be consumed at any time of day, but it is particularly delicious for breakfast or as a post-workout drink. It is ideal for those attempting to lose weight, gain muscle, or keep a healthy diet.

Prep Time: 10 Minutes

Total Time: 10 Minutes

Serving: 1

Ingredients

- 1 cup of fresh or frozen strawberries
- 1/2 frozen banana, chopped into chunks
- 1 tbsp chocolate or vanilla protein powder
- 1 tbsp raw cacao powder or cocoa powder
- 1 1/4 cup of unsweetened almond milk or other non-dairy milk
- 2 pitted medjool dates
- 1/2 tspvanilla
- 4-5 cubes of ice
- 2 drops of stevia to sweeten (optional)

Instructions

1. Add the strawberries, banana, protein powder, cacao powder, almond milk, dates, and vanilla into a blender. Blend until the fruit is pureed.
2. Add the ice cubes to the blender and blend until the mixture is smooth.
3. Taste the smoothie and add stevia if desired.
4. Pour the smoothie into a T-shaped glass and enjoy!

33. CHOCOLATE HAZELNUT SMOOTHIE

The Chocolate Hazelnut Smoothie is a nutrient-rich and tasty beverage that is perfect for people who want to maintain good health. It is high in antioxidants, vitamins, and minerals, making it a good option for those with health concerns. The smoothie is suitable for any time of day and can be consumed as a meal replacement or snack. It is ideal for people who are lactose intolerant or vegan, as it does not contain dairy products. The Chocolate Hazelnut Smoothie is made with hazelnuts, raw cacao powder, dates, and vanilla extract, making it a delicious and healthy treat.

Prep Time: 5 Minutes

Total Time: 5 Minutes

Serving: 1

Ingredients

- 3/4 cup of (6 ounces) water
- 1/4 cup of (35 grams) whole hazelnuts (with or without skin)
- 1 heaping tbsp (7 grams) raw cacao powder
- 4 pitted Medjool dates (73 grams)
- 1/4 tsp(1 gram) vanilla extract
- 6 large ice cubes

Instructions

1. Combine water, hazelnuts, cacao powder, dates, and vanilla extract in a high-speed blender.
2. Blend the mixture until smooth. If you taste the mixture now, keep in mind that the flavor will become diluted when you add ice.
3. Add the ice cubes to the blender and blend again until the mixture reaches a slushy texture. Note that if you use less ice, the flavor will be more concentrated, and if you use more ice, the flavor will be more diluted.
4. Serve the Chocolate Hazelnut Smoothie right away for the best taste and texture.

34. CHOCOLATE CHIP MINT SMOOTHIE

The Chocolate Chip Mint Smoothie is a healthy and nutritious drink made with coconut milk, Greek yogurt, spinach, frozen bananas, whey protein, and dark chocolate. It is high in protein, fiber, and other important nutrients. The smoothie can be enjoyed as a meal replacement or a snack at any time of the day. The refreshing peppermint extract provides a natural energy boost, while the dark chocolate chunks add a delicious flavor and texture. This smoothie is perfect for anyone who wants to maintain a healthy and balanced diet while satisfying their cravings for a sweet and delicious treat. It is also an excellent choice for those who are lactose intolerant, as it contains no dairy.

Prep Time: 5 Minutes

Total Time: 5 Minutes

Serving: 1

Ingredients

- 1/2 cup of full-fat canned coconut milk
- 1/2 cup of Greek yogurt or plain Greek yogurt
- 2 bananas, chopped and frozen
- 4 cups of fresh or frozen spinach and 6 ice cubes
- 20 grams of unsweetened and unflavored whey
- 1 tspof vanilla
- 1/2-1 tspof peppermint extract
- 2 tbsp of chopped 85% dark chocolate

Instructions

1. Start by adding the liquid ingredients, such as the coconut milk and Greek yogurt, into a blender.
2. Next, add the frozen chopped bananas, fresh or frozen spinach, whey protein, vanilla, and peppermint extract into the blender.
3. Process the ingredients until the mixture is smooth and creamy, and the spinach is fully blended.
4. Once the mixture is smooth, add the chopped dark chocolate into the blender and pulse 5-6 times until the chocolate is broken up but still in chunks.
5. Pour the smoothie into a glass and top with additional dark chocolate chips, if desired.
6. Enjoy the chocolate chip mint smoothie while it's thick and creamy.

35. CHOCOLATE RASPBERRY CHEESECAKE SMOOTHIE

The "Chocolate Raspberry Cheesecake Smoothie" is a delicious and healthy drink that has numerous benefits for those who consume it. Firstly, it is a low-calorie and dairy-free option, which is perfect for individuals who want to maintain a healthy and balanced diet. Secondly, the smoothie contains whey protein isolate, which is essential for muscle growth and repair. Additionally, the fresh or frozen raspberries used in the smoothie are packed with antioxidants, vitamins, and fiber, providing a range of health benefits.

The "Chocolate Raspberry Cheesecake Smoothie" is a versatile drink that can be taken at any time of day. It is an ideal breakfast or mid-day snack, as it is both delicious and nutritious. It is also an excellent post-workout drink, helping with muscle recovery and growth.

Prep Time: 5 Minutes

Total Time: 5 Minutes

Serving: 1

Ingredients

- 1 cup of unsweetened almond milk
- 2 tbsp of cream cheese
- 1 ounce (32/3 tablespoons) of fresh or frozen raspberries
- ¼ tspof vanilla extract
- ¼ tspof stevia drops
- ¼ cup of (¾ ounce) of unflavored whey protein isolate
- 1 tbsp of cocoa powder
- 1 cup of ice cubes
- ¼ cup of heavy whipping cream or coconut cream (optional)

Instructions

1. Combine almond milk, cream cheese, raspberries, vanilla extract, and stevia drops in a blender. Blend the ingredients until they are mixed.
2. Add unflavored whey protein isolate, cocoa powder, and ice cubes to the blender. For creamier texture, include heavy whipping cream or coconut cream.
3. Blend everything until you get a smooth and creamy consistency.
4. Serve the smoothie immediately and enjoy!

36. CHOCOLATE RASPBERRY SMOOTHIE

"Chocolate Raspberry Smoothie" is a delicious and healthy beverage that can be consumed at any time of the day. It is an excellent source of nutrients such as protein, fiber, antioxidants, and vitamins. The smoothie is perfect for people who are looking to maintain a healthy diet or lose weight. The unsweetened almond milk and zero-calorie sweetener make it a great option for those with diabetes or those who want to reduce their sugar intake. The smoothie is also a great post-workout drink as it contains chocolate protein powder, which can help in muscle recovery.

Prep Time: 5 Minutes

Total Time: 5 Minutes

Serving: 1

Ingredients

- 12 ounces of unsweetened almond milk
- 1 ½ tbsp of unsweetened cocoa powder
- 1 scoop of chocolate protein powder
- ½ of a frozen banana
- ½ cup of frozen raspberries
- ½ tspof Born Sweet Zing™ Zero Calorie Stevia Sweetener (adjust to taste)
- A handful of ice
- Berries, cacao nibs, or dark chocolate chips (optional, for garnish)

Instructions

1. Add all ingredients (except for the garnish) to a blender.
2. Blend until the components are smooth and well combined.
3. Sweetness can be adjusted to taste by adding more or less Born Sweet ZingTM Zero Calorie Stevia Sweetener.
4. If the smoothie is too viscous, thin it out with more almond milk. If it's too thin, add more ice to make it thicker.
5. Once the smoothie has reached your desired consistency, pour it into a glass.
6. If you choose to add a garnish, sprinkle some berries, cacao nibs, or dark chocolate chips on top of the smoothie.
7. Serve the chocolate raspberry smoothie immediately and enjoy!

37. DETOXIFYING BEET & BERRY SMOOTHIE

The Detoxifying Beet & Berry Smoothie is high in minerals that are beneficial to your health. Beets are rich in antioxidants and anti-inflammatory properties, which may help lower the risk of chronic diseases. Berries, on the other hand, are high in fiber and vitamin C, both of which aid metabolism and strengthen the immune system. Because of the nitrates contained in beets, this smoothie can also help improve blood circulation and lower blood pressure.

This smoothie is perfect for any time of the day, but it's especially beneficial to drink in the morning as a breakfast or mid-day snack. Drinking it in the morning can help jump-start your digestion and give you the energy you need to start your day. It's also a great way to keep hydrated throughout the day.

The Detoxifying Beet & Berry Smoothie is ideal for anyone looking to better their health and well-being. It's a wonderful option for those who want to eat more fruits and vegetables but find it difficult to do so raw. It's also a great way to detoxify the body and support healthy digestion. Additionally, it's vegan, gluten-free, and dairy-free, making it suitable for people with dietary restrictions.

Prep Time: 5 Minutes

Total Time: 5 Minutes

Serving: 2

Ingredients

- 1/3 cup of peeled and chopped raw beet (organic when possible)
- 1 ⅓ cup of frozen strawberries (if fresh, add ice // organic when possible)
- 1/4 ripe frozen banana (optional // peeled and sliced)
- 2/3 cup of fresh apple juice (recipe in our cookbook!)
- Fresh mint or shredded coconut (for garnish // optional)

Instructions

1. Gather all the ingredients and prepare them as needed.
2. Add the peeled and chopped raw beet, frozen strawberries, ripe frozen banana (optional for sweetness), and fresh apple juice to a blender.
3. Blend everything on high until the mixture is smooth and creamy. Make sure to scrape the blender's sides as needed.
4. Taste the smoothie and adjust the flavor as needed. Add more banana for sweetness, apple juice to thin the consistency, or more strawberries for a more intense fruit flavor.
5. Once you're satisfied with the taste, divide the smoothie between two serving glasses.
6. Garnish the smoothie with fresh mint or shredded coconut, if desired.
7. Serve and enjoy your Detoxifying Beet & Berry Smoothie!

38. CUCUMBER MINT SMOOTHIE

Cucumber mint smoothie is a great way to boost your immune system and improve digestion. Cucumbers are full of fiber and water, which help keep your bowels moving well and keep you from getting constipated. Mint leaves are known for their cooling and soothing properties, which can aid in reducing inflammation and ease digestive problems. This smoothie is also low in calories and high in antioxidants, which makes it a great choice for people trying to lose weight.

A cucumber mint smoothie is a refreshing beverage that can be try on at any time of the day. It makes for a refreshing breakfast or a mid-day snack, and it can also be consumed after a workout to replenish your body's nutrients.

Cucumber mint smoothie is perfect for people who are looking for a healthy and low-calorie drink that is easy to make. It is a great option for those who want to add more fruits and vegetables to their diet without compromising on taste. Serve the smoothie directly in a glass.

Prep Time: 5 Minutes

Total Time: 5 Minutes

Serving: 1

Ingredients:

- 1 cucumber, sliced (fresh or frozen)
- 1/4 cup-3/4 cup unsweetened vanilla almond milk (1/4 cup if using fresh cucumber, 3/4 cup if using frozen cucumber)
- 3 large mint leaves
- 1 scoop MegaFood Daily Energy Nutrient Booster Powder
- 1/2 tsppure stevia powder
- 1 cup of ice

Instructions

1. Slice the cucumber into small pieces if using fresh cucumber. If using frozen cucumber, allow it to thaw slightly.
2. Add the sliced cucumber, almond milk, mint leaves, nutrient booster powder, stevia powder, and ice to a blender.
3. Mix all the ingredients until the mixture is creamy and smooth.
4. If the smoothie isn't sweet enough, add more stevia powder to make it sweeter.
5. Pour the smoothie into a T-shaped glass and enjoy!

39. GOLDEN MILK SMOOTHIE RECIPE

Golden Milk Smoothie is a healthy and delicious beverage that offers numerous health benefits. The smoothie contains ground cinnamon, turmeric, ginger, and black pepper that are all known for their anti-inflammatory properties. These ingredients also aid in digestion, boost immunity, and improve brain function. The smoothie is also rich in protein and calcium due to the Greek yogurt and almond milk, making it a great option for post-workout recovery.

The best time to enjoy a Golden Milk Smoothie is in the morning or after a workout. The smoothie is perfect for anyone looking for a healthy and tasty alternative to traditional smoothies. It is also an excellent option for individuals with dietary restrictions, as it can be easily adapted to be dairy-free.

Prep Time: 5 Minutes

Total Time: 5 Minutes

Serving: 1

Ingredients

- 1 cup of frozen mango chunks
- ½ frozen banana
- 1/2 cup of plain Greek yogurt (use a dairy-free substitute if needed)
- 1/2 tspground cinnamon
- 1/2 tspground turmeric or 1 Tbsp peeled and grated fresh turmeric
- 1/4 tspground ginger or 1/2 Tbsp peeled and grated fresh ginger
- 1 cup of unsweetened vanilla almond milk (or your favorite milk)
- Pinch of black pepper
-

Instructions

1. Add all the ingredients into a high-powered blender.
2. Blend the mixture until smooth and creamy.
3. Pour the smoothie into a glass.
4. Enjoy the Golden Milk Smoothie immediately after making.

40. GREEN APPLE SMOOTHIE

Green Apple Smoothie is a delicious and healthy drink you can enjoy any time of day. This smoothie is packed with nutrients from baby spinach, frozen fruits, fresh apple, and honey and is a great way to integrate more fruits and veggies into your diet. The inclusion of chia, hemp, or flax seeds increases the amount of omega-3 fatty acids, fiber, and protein.

This smoothie is perfect for anyone looking for a quick and easy breakfast or a refreshing snack throughout the day. It is also an excellent option for people who are trying to maintain a healthy lifestyle or are following a vegan or plant-based diet. The smoothie can be consumed directly after blending and used as a meal replacement or supplement to a healthy diet.

Total Time: 5 Minutes

Serving: 2

Ingredients

- 1 cup of baby spinach (packed)
- 3/4 cup of plain unsweetened almond milk or water, divided (plus more to thin if necessary)
- 1 small frozen banana (about 1/2 cup of frozen banana slices)
- 1/2 cup of pineapple chunks, frozen (or use mango, peaches or more banana)
- 1/2 cup of fresh apple diced (approximately 1/2 an apple; I used a Granny Smith)
- 1 tbsp freshly squeezed lemon juice
- 1 tbsp honey (or other liquid sweetener such as maple syrup or agave nectar),
- Optional: a handful of ice cubes
- Optional 1 tspchia seeds, hemp seeds, or flax seeds

Instructions

1. In a blender, add spinach and 1/2 cup of almond milk or water. Blend until smooth. (This helps to avoid any spinach chunks in the smoothie.)
2. Add the frozen banana, frozen pineapple or other fruit, diced apple, lemon juice, honey, 1/4 cup of remaining almond milk and ice cubes (and any add-ins like seeds) to the blender.
3. Blend the contents until it is smooth and creamy.Check if the smoothie is too thick, add more almond milk or water until the right consistency is reached.Serve immediately.

41. GREEN GODDESS SMOOTHIE

Green Goddess Smoothie is a healthy and nutritious drink that is ideal for health-conscious individuals who wish to incorporate more greens into their diet. The green apples, kale or spinach, and flaxseeds in this smoothie are high in minerals and antioxidants, which can help boost immunity, improve digestion, and support general health.

The addition of peanut butter and almond milk provides healthy fats and protein, making it a filling and satisfying drink. The natural sweetness from the maple syrup and banana makes it a tasty and refreshing drink.

This smoothie is best consumed in the morning as a breakfast drink or as a mid-day snack to provide sustained energy throughout the day. It is also great for people who are on a plant-based or vegan diet.

Prep Time: 5 Minutes

Serving: 2

Ingredients

- 2 green apples
- 1 frozen banana (fresh banana can also be used)
- 2 cups of either kale or spinach
- 4 tbsp of peanut butter
- 2 tbsp of flaxseeds
- 2 tbsp of maple syrup
- 2 cups of almond milk

Instructions

1. Wash the green apples and remove their cores. Cut them into small chunks.
2. Next, peel the banana and cut it into small pieces.
3. Rinse the kale or spinach and remove any tough stems.
4. Add the chopped green apples, banana, kale or spinach, peanut butter, flaxseeds, and maple syrup to a blender.
5. Pour in the almond milk.
6. Blend all the ingredients together until smooth and creamy.
7. Add a little more almond milk and blend again if the drink is too thick.
8. Once smooth, pour the green goddess smoothie into glasses.
9. Serve immediately and enjoy your delicious and nutritious green goddess smoothie!

42. GREEN MACHINE SMOOTHIE

The Orange Carrot Ginger Smoothie is a healthy and nutritious drink perfect for people who want to improve their health. It's packed with vitamins and minerals that can enhance immune function, support better digestion, and encourage healthy skin.

This smoothie is a great choice for a quick breakfast or snack, and it's best to drink it in the morning to start your day off right. It's ideal for people who want to add more fruits and vegetables to their diet.

Ingredients

- 1 cup of baby spinach leaves (packed)
- 1 cup of frozen pineapple chunks
- 1/2 large apple or 1 small apple (seeds removed and cut into chunks)
- 1/4 large ripe avocado or 1/2 small ripe avocado
- 1-inch chunk that will be fresh ginger (no need to peel)
- 1/2 cup of coconut water (plus more if needed)
- 1/4 lemon (juiced)
- Dash of cayenne pepper

Instructions

1. Place the packed baby spinach leaves and 1/2 cup of coconut water in a high-powered blender. Blend until the greens are completely liquified.
2. Add the frozen pineapple chunks, apple chunks, ginger, avocado, lemon juice, and a dash of cayenne pepper to the blender.
3. Blend everything on high until the mixture is smooth.
4. Check the consistency and sweetness of the smoothie. If it's too thick, add more coconut water to thin it out. If it's not sweet enough, add more frozen pineapple or your preferred sweetener.
5. Once the smoothie reaches your desired consistency and sweetness, serve it immediately.

43. GREEN MONSTER SMOOTHIE

The Green Monster Smoothie recipe is a healthy and delicious way to start your day. Packed with nutrients, this smoothie is perfect for anyone looking to boost their intake of greens. The recipe includes spinach, which is high in vitamins A and C, fiber, and antioxidants.

The addition of Greek yogurt provides a good source of protein, and the frozen Banana gives the smoothie a sweet, creamy taste. This smoothie is perfect for a quick breakfast or as a mid-day snack. Additionally, it's an excellent choice for those seeking a lactose-free and gluten-free substitute.

Prep Time: 5 Minutes

Total Time: 5 Minutes

Serving: 1

Ingredients

- 1 cup of plain or vanilla coconut milk
- 6-8 ounce of vanilla Greek yogurt
- 1 ripe frozen banana
- 2-4 cups of raw, organic spinach (I prefer 3 cups)

Instructions

1. Add all of the cooking ingredients into a blender.
2. Bled the mixture until it is completely smooth and has a creamy consistency.
3. If the mixture is too thick, Incorporate additional coconut milk to achieve the preferred thickness.
4. Pour it into a glass and enjoy!

44. GREEN TEA MATCHA SMOOTHIE

Green Tea Matcha Smoothie is a refreshing and healthy beverage that is perfect for anyone looking to boost their energy levels and improve their health. This smoothie is packed with nutritious ingredients like baby spinach, baby kale, Banana, and almonds, as well as matcha green tea powder, which is high in antioxidants and provides a natural caffeine boost. It is a great option for breakfast or as a pre-workout drink. This smoothie is also low in calories and sugar, making it a suitable choice for those For individuals monitoring their weight or aiming to regulate their blood glucose levels.

Prep Time: 5 Minutes

Total Time: 5 Minutes

Serving: 2

Ingredients

- 2 cups of ice cubes
- 1 cup of unsweetened almond milk
- ½ cup of nonfat plain Greek yogurt or dairy-free alternative
- 1 cup of baby spinach
- 1 cup of baby kale
- 1 sliced banana
- ¼ cup of sliced almonds
- 1 tbsp matcha green tea powder
- 2 tsp natural sweetener, such as Truvia® Natural Sweetener

Instructions

1. Add all ingredients, including ice cubes, almond milk, Greek yogurt, baby spinach, baby kale, sliced Banana, sliced almonds, matcha green tea powder, and natural sweetener, into a blender.
2. Blend the mixture for 60 to 90 seconds until it becomes smooth. If you prefer a thicker smoothie, add more ice. If you prefer a thinner smoothie, add more milk.
3. Transfer the smoothie to a glass and enjoy it right away.

45. KALE BANANA GREEN SMOOTHIE

The Kale Banana Green Smoothie is a healthy and nutritious drink that can provide many benefits. Kale is high in fiber and antioxidants, while Banana provides a good source of potassium and vitamin C. The addition of flax seeds adds omega-3 fatty acids and maple syrup provides a natural sweetener. This smoothie is perfect for anyone looking to add more greens and nutrients to their diet. This can be enjoyed at any moment throughout the day., but it's particularly good as a breakfast or mid-morning snack.

Prep Time: 5 Minutes

Total Time: 5 Minutes

Serving: 1

Ingredients:

- 2 cups of chopped kale
- 1 banana
- ½ cup of light unsweetened soy milk
- 1 tbsp flax seeds
- 1 tspmaple syrup

Instructions

1. Wash the kale leaves thoroughly and chop them into small pieces.
2. The Banana should be peeled and cut into tiny pieces.
3. Add the chopped kale and Banana to a blender.
4. Pour in the light unsweetened soy milk.
5. Add the flax seeds and maple syrup to the blender.
6. Cover the blender and blend all the ingredients until the mixture is smooth and creamy.
7. Add a little more soy milk and blend the drink once more if it is too thin.
8. Pour the smoothie into a glass serve over ice.

46. KALE PINEAPPLE SMOOTHIE

This Kale Pineapple Smoothie recipe is a healthy and refreshing drink that's perfect for anyone looking for a nutrient-packed beverage. The kale provides a dose of vitamins and minerals, while the pineapple adds a sweet and tangy flavor, as well as more nutrients like vitamin C and bromelain. The addition of Greek yogurt and peanut butter adds protein and healthy fats, making this smoothie a great post-workout drink or breakfast option. The recipe is also customizable, as you can adjust the sweetness to your liking with honey. It's best to drink this smoothie immediately after blending to get the maximum nutritional benefits.

Prep Time: 4 Minutes

Total Time: 4 Minutes

Serving: 2

Ingredients

- 2 cups chopped kale leaves with stems removed, loosely packed 3/4 cup vanilla almond milk without added sugar (or any preferred milk variety)
- 1 medium banana, frozen and cut into chunks
- 1/4 cup of plain nonfat Greek yogurt
- 1/4 cup of frozen pineapple pieces
- 2 tbsp creamy or crunchy peanut butter (I use natural creamy)
- 1 to 3 tsp honey to taste

Instructions

1. In the sequence mentioned, add the following ingredients to a blender: kale, almond milk, Banana, yogurt, pineapple, peanut butter, and honey.
2. The mixture should be smooth; if more milk is required to achieve the desired consistency, apply it.
3. Drink the smoothie right away after pouring it into a tumbler.

47. KEY LIME PIE SMOOTHIE

This Key Lime Pie Smoothie recipe is a delicious and healthy option for breakfast or a refreshing snack. The combination of frozen Banana, Greek yogurt, lime juice, honey, and lime zest provides a rich source of vitamins, minerals, and antioxidants that support overall health. It is a perfect drink for those who prefer a tangy and sweet flavor. The smoothie is ideal for people who are lactose intolerant and can substitute Greek yogurt with a dairy-free alternative. It is also perfect for individuals who want to maintain a healthy and balanced diet while enjoying a tasty treat.

Prep Time: 5 Minutes

Total Time: 5 Minutes

Serving: 1

Ingredients

- 1 frozen banana, sliced
- ½ cup of plain Greek yogurt (130 g) or dairy-free alternative
- ¼ cup of key lime juice or lime juice (60 mL)
- 1 tbsp of honey (15 mL) or sweetener of choice
- ½ tspof finely grated lime zest
- ¼ tspof vanilla extract (1.2 mL)
- Optional for texture: ice
- Optional for color: fresh spinach leaves
- Optional garnish: graham cracker crumbs, lime wedge

Instructions

1. Add the frozen Banana, Greek yogurt, lime juice, honey, lime zest, and vanilla extract to a blender.
2. When necessary, add ice to the mixture as you blend all the components to the desired consistency. Add a few raw spinach leaves to your smoothie if you prefer it to be slightly green.
3. The rim of the drink should be rubbed with lime juice before being covered in crushed graham cracker crumbs as a garnish.
4. Pour the smoothie into the glass and serve immediately.

48. KIWI STRAWBERRY SMOOTHIE

The Kiwi Strawberry Smoothie is a delicious and nutritious drink that can be enjoyed any time of day. Packed with vitamin C, fiber, and antioxidants from fruits, this smoothie is great for boosting immune health, improving digestion, and promoting glowing skin. The addition of vanilla frozen yogurt gives it a creamy and satisfying texture, making it a perfect breakfast or post-workout snack. This smoothie is also low in calories and fat, making it a great option for anyone looking to maintain a healthy diet. It is particularly suited for those who enjoy fruity and refreshing drinks.

Prep Time: 5 Minutes

Total Time: 5 Minutes

Serving: 1

Ingredients

- 3/4 cup of pineapple and orange juice blend
- 1/2 cup of vanilla frozen yogurt
- 1 banana
- 6 strawberries
- 1 kiwi

Instructions

1. Peel and chop the Banana into small pieces. Rinse and hull the strawberries, and slice the kiwi into small chunks.
2. Blend the liquid mixture with the frozen yogurt, Banana, strawberries, and kiwi.
3. Blend at a high pace just until the mixture becomes creamy and smooth.
4. Serve the smoothie right away by pouring it into two cups of.

49. LEMON BLUEBERRY SMOOTHIE

The Lemon Blueberry Smoothie recipe offers a nutritious and invigorating beverage, ideal for a speedy breakfast or snack time. The smoothie is packed with antioxidants, fiber, and essential vitamins and minerals from blueberries and lemon, This makes it an ideal choice for anyone in search of a nourishing beverage. The almond extract and dairy-free milk add a creamy texture to the smoothie while also making it suitable for individuals who are lactose intolerant or follow a vegan diet. This smoothie can be enjoyed at any time of the day and is a great option for those who are looking for a tasty and healthy beverage.

Prep Time: 5 Minutes

Total Time: 5 Minutes

Serving: 1

Ingredients

- 1 cup of frozen blueberries (or mixed berries)
- 1 frozen ripe banana
- 1/2 lemon, juiced (about 2 tbsp fresh lemon juice)
- Zest from 1 lemon
- 1/8 tspalmond extract
- 1/2 cup dairy-free milk of choice, plus more to thin if necessary

Instructions

1. In a large, high-powered blender, add all the ingredients, including frozen blueberries, frozen Banana, fresh lemon juice, lemon zest, almond extract, and 1/2 cup of dairy-free milk of choice.
2. Blend until when all the ingredients are well combined and the mixture is smooth.
3. Should the smoothie be overly thick, incorporate more dairy-free milk to achieve the preferred consistency and blend once more.
4. Pour the smoothie into a glass and garnish with additional lemon zest, blueberries, and granola if desired.
5. Enjoy your refreshing and delicious Lemon Blueberry Smoothie!

50. RASPBERRY LEMONADE SMOOTHIE

This Raspberry Lemonade Smoothie recipe is a delicious and healthy beverage option that can be eaten any time of the day. The combination of frozen red raspberries, nonfat Greek yogurt, almond milk, fresh lemon juice, and pure maple syrup makes for a nutrient-dense and refreshing drink. The smoothie is high in antioxidants, vitamins, and minerals, which help to support a healthy immune system and improve overall health. This recipe is perfect for anyone looking for a quick and easy way to increase their fruit and yogurt intake. Whether it's for breakfast, a mid-day snack, or post-workout fuel, this smoothie is a perfect choice for a healthy and satisfying drink.

Prep Time: 5 Minutes

Total Time: 5 Minutes

Serving: 1

Ingredients

- 1 cup of frozen red raspberries
- 4 ounces of nonfat Greek yogurt
- ¼ cup of almond milk
- 1 tbsp of fresh lemon juice
- 1 tbsp of pure maple syrup
- Additional red raspberries for garnish

Instructions

1. Add the frozen red raspberries, nonfat Greek yogurt, almond milk, fresh lemon juice, and pure maple syrup to a blender or use a handheld immersion blender to combine all the ingredients.
2. Process the ingredients until they become smooth and creamy.
3. Pour the smoothie into a glass and garnish with additional red raspberries.
4. Serve and enjoy!

51. MANGO BANANA COCONUT SMOOTHIE

This recipe for a mango, Banana, and coconut smoothie is a light, nutritious beverage that goes well with any meal or snack. Packed with nutritious ingredients like frozen mango, Banana, shredded coconut, hemp hearts, coconut-flavored Greek yogurt, and milk, This smoothie serves as an excellent kickstart to your day or a rejuvenating post-workout refreshment. The combination of fruit and coconut gives it a sweet tropical flavor that will satisfy your cravings without added sugars. This smoothie is also a great source of protein, healthy fats, and fiber, making it an excellent choice for those looking for a healthy and filling meal replacement. Perfect for anyone who wants a delicious and healthy drink that is easy to make and enjoy!

Prep Time: 10 Minutes

Total Time: 10 Minutes

Serving: 2

Ingredients

- 1 cup of frozen mango chunks (or a combination of mango and pineapple chunks)
- 1 frozen banana it will be peeled and cut into chunks
- 1 tbsp shredded coconut
- 1/4 cup of hemp hearts
- 3/4 cup of coconut-flavored Greek yogurt
- 3/4 cup of milk of choice (coconut beverage is recommended)

Instructions

1. Add all ingredients to a high-quality blender.
2. Blend on high until smooth and creamy, scraping down the sides as needed.
3. In case the smoothie is excessively thick, gradually add more milk in small amounts until you achieve the preferred consistency.
4. Pour into glasses and serve immediately. Enjoy your Mango Banana Coconut Smoothie!

52. MANGO GREEN TEA SMOOTHIE

This Mango Green Tea Smoothie is a refreshing and healthy drink that combines the natural sweetness of mango with the antioxidant properties of green tea. It's a great way to start your day or as a mid-day snack. This smoothie is perfect for anyone who wants to boost their immune system, improve digestion, or simply enjoy a delicious and healthy drink. The addition of honey is optional for those who prefer a sweeter taste. Enjoy this smoothie in the morning or afternoon for a natural energy boost.

Prep Time: 10 Minutes

Total Time: 10 Minutes

Serving: 4

Ingredients

- 2 ripe mangoes
- 1 cup of hot boiling water
- 2 green tea bags
- 2 cups of ice
- 1/2 frozen banana
- Honey (optional)

Instructions

1. Begin by adding 2 green tea bags to 1 cup of boiling water. Allow the tea bags to steep in the water for a few minutes, and then place the tea in the freezer to cool while you prepare the rest of the smoothie.
2. While the tea cools, peel the ripe mangoes, remove the pit, and add the flesh to the blender. Then, add 2 cups of ice, 1/2 frozen banana, and 1 tbsp of honey if you prefer a sweeter smoothie.
3. Once the green tea has cooled down, remove the tea bags from the tea and discard them. Pour the tea into the blender and cover the blender.
4. Puree the mixture until it becomes smooth. Make sure to regularly scrape down the blender's edges.
5. When the mixture is smooth, pour it into glasses and serve immediately. Enjoy your delicious Mango Green Tea Smoothie!

53. MANGO PINEAPPLE COCONUT SMOOTHIE

The Mango Pineapple Coconut Smoothie is a delicious and healthy drink that's perfect for any time of day. This smoothie is loaded with essential vitamins, minerals, and antioxidants from the mango, pineapple, and coconut and is a fantastic supply of good fats thanks to almond milk.

The optional almonds and flax seeds also add an extra boost of protein and fiber to keep you feeling full and satisfied. This smoothie is especially great for people who are looking to improve their digestion, boost their immune system, and increase their energy levels.

It's best to drink this smoothie immediately after blending to enjoy its maximum nutritional benefits.

Prep Time: 5 Minutes

Total Time: 5 Minutes

Serving: 2

Ingredients

- 1 cup of Almond Breeze Original or Unsweetened Original almond milk
- 1 cup of fresh or frozen mango cubes
- 1 cup of fresh, frozen, or juice-packed pineapple chunks
- Optional: 1 tbsp toasted slivered or sliced almonds
- Optional: 1 tspground flax seeds

Instructions

1. Add the almond milk, mango cubes, and pineapple chunks to a blender.
2. If using, add the optional toasted almonds and ground flax seeds.
3. Pure all ingredients in the blender until smooth and creamy.
4. Pour the smoothie into a glass.
5. Serve and enjoy immediately.

54. MANGO PINEAPPLE SMOOTHIE

Mango Pineapple Smoothie is a delicious and refreshing drink packed with health benefits. This smoothie is perfect for those who want to boost their immune system and maintain good health. The combination of mango and pineapple provides a good dose of vitamin C, while coconut or almond milk offers a healthy source of fat. It's best to drink this smoothie in the morning as a breakfast meal or as a post-workout recovery drink. This smoothie is also a great option for vegans and those with lactose intolerance.

Prep Time: 5 Minutes

Total Time: 5 Minutes

Serving: 1

Ingredients

- ¾ cup of frozen mango chunks
- ½ cup of fresh pineapple chunks
- ½ small frozen Banana cut into pieces
- 1 ¼ cup of coconut milk or almond milk
- ½ cup of ice

Instructions

Add all of the smoothie ingredients to the jug of a blender.

Blend the ingredients on high speed until smooth. If the smoothie turns out too thick, feel free to dilute it by incorporating a bit more milk or water.

Once the smoothie is blended to your desired consistency, pour it into glasses and serve immediately.

55. MANGO STRAWBERRY COCONUT SMOOTHIE

Mango Strawberry Coconut Smoothie is a healthy and refreshing drink packed with vitamins, minerals, and antioxidants. It is perfect for anyone looking to improve their overall health and well-being. The best time to drink this smoothie is in the morning or as a post-workout snack. It is especially great for people who are looking to boost their immune system, improve digestion, or maintain a healthy weight.

Prep Time: 5 Minutes

Total Time: 5 Minutes

Serving: 2

Ingredients

- 1 medium-sized banana, peeled, sliced, and frozen
- 1 cup of sweetened coconut milk
- 1 mango, peeled and cut of into chunks
- 5 large strawberries (around 3.5cm in diameter)

Instructions

1. Take the frozen banana slices out of the freezer and let them thaw for a few minutes until they soften slightly.
2. Add the thawed banana slices, sweetened coconut milk, mango chunks, and strawberries to a blender.
3. Blend the ingredients on high speed until the mixture is completely smooth and no chunks remain.
4. Dispense the smoothie into a glass and enjoy it right away. Enjoy your delicious and refreshing Mango Strawberry Coconut Smoothie!

56. MANGO TANGO SMOOTHIE

The Mango Tango Smoothie is a scrumptious and nutritious beverage suitable for any moment throughout the day. With its combination of mango, Banana, milk, yogurt, and pineapple juice, this smoothie is packed with essential vitamins, minerals, and antioxidants. It's a great way to boost your energy and maintain good health. The smoothie is ideal for people who are looking for a nutritious and refreshing drink that is low in fat and calories. It's best consumed immediately after preparation to get the most out of its nutritional benefits.

Prep Time: 5 Minutes

Total Time: 5 Minutes

Serving: 2

Ingredients

- 1 cup of chopped peeled mango
- 1 medium ripe banana, frozen, peeled, and sliced
- 1 cup of fat-free milk
- 1/2 cup of reduced-fat plain yogurt
- 1/2 cup of unsweetened pineapple juice

Instructions

1. Begin by adding all of the ingredients to a blender.
2. Cover the blender and process the mixture until it's completely smooth.
3. When the mixture is smooth, pour it into chilled glasses.
4. Serve the smoothie immediately, and enjoy!

57. MANGO TURMERIC SMOOTHIE

This Mango Turmeric Smoothie recipe is a healthy and flavorful drink that's perfect for any time of the day. It's loaded with nutrients and antioxidants from the mango, Banana, orange, ginger, and turmeric, which may aid in decreasing inflammation, enhancing immune function, and promoting better digestion. The addition of soy milk and non-dairy yogurt also makes it a great option for vegans or those with lactose intolerance. This smoothie is best consumed in the morning as a healthy breakfast option or as a refreshing midday snack. It's perfect for anyone looking for a nutritious and delicious drink to add to their diet.

Prep Time: 5 Minutes

Total Time: 5 Minutes

Serving: 2

Ingredients

- 1 1/2 cups of frozen, cubed mango
- 1 frozen banana
- 1/2 cup of plain, unsweetened soy milk
- 1/2 cup of plain, non-dairy yogurt
- 1/2 orange, peeled and supremed
- 1/2 inch peeled fresh ginger (or 1 tspground ginger)
- 1/2 inch peeled turmeric root (or 1/2 tspground turmeric)

Instructions

1. Add all the ingredients to a blender.
2. Puree the mixture until smooth.
3. To obtain the desired consistency, add more water or soy milk if the smoothie is too thick.
4. Serve the smoothie right away after pouring it into a tumbler.
5. Enjoy your delicious Mango Turmeric Smoothie!

58. MINT CHOCOLATE CHIP SMOOTHIE

This Mint Chocolate Chip Smoothie recipe is a delicious and healthy drink that's perfect for anyone looking for a refreshing and nutritious beverage. Packed with fresh spinach, avocado, and mint leaves, this smoothie is loaded with vitamins and minerals. It's also a great source of protein, thanks to the addition of vanilla protein powder or collagen peptides. This smoothie is delightful at any time, especially as a breakfast option or a post-exercise snack. It's ideal for those seeking a delicious indulgence while maintaining a health-conscious lifestyle.

Prep Time: 5 Minutes

Total Time: 5 Minutes

Serving: 1

Ingredients

- 1 small frozen banana
- 1 ½ cups of unsweetened vanilla almond milk
- 1 cup of fresh spinach
- ¼ small/medium-sized avocado
- 20-30 fresh mint leaves
- 1 scoop vanilla protein powder or collagen peptides
- ½ cup of crushed ice (or more for a thicker smoothie)
- 1 tbsp cacao nibs or chocolate chips
- Whipped cream or whipped coconut cream (optional, for garnish)

Instructions

1. Place the frozen Banana, almond milk, spinach, avocado, mint leaves, protein powder, or collagen peptides, and crushed ice into a blender.
2. Process the mixture until smooth.
3. Add in the cacao nibs or chocolate chips and stir or pulse briefly (do not over-puree, or the smoothie will turn brown).
4. Serve immediately, garnished with whipped cream or coconut cream and additional cacao nibs or chocolate chips if desired. Enjoy!

59. MINT MANGO SMOOTHIE

Mint Mango Smoothie is a refreshing and nutritious drink that's perfect for anyone looking to boost their energy levels and get a healthy dose of vitamins and minerals. This smoothie contains frozen mango, mint leaves, Greek yogurt, and milk, making it a good source of protein, fiber, and antioxidants. It's a great drink for breakfast or a midday snack and can be enjoyed by anyone who wants a tasty and healthy beverage. Additionally, The inclusion of fresh mint leaves in this smoothie can assist with digestion and alleviate inflammation, rendering it an excellent option. A great choice for anyone with digestive issues or inflammation-related conditions.

Prep Time: 5 Minutes

Total Time: 5 Minutes

Serving: 1

Ingredients

- 1 1/2 cups of frozen mango
- 4-5 mint leaves
- 1 cup of milk
- 3/4 cup of whole milk Greek yogurt

Instructions

1. Add all the ingredients to a high-speed blender.
2. Blend the ingredients until they are completely smooth.
3. If desired, garnish the smoothie with a fresh mint leaf before serving.

60. MIXED BERRY SMOOTHIE

The Mixed Berry Smoothie Recipe is a tasty and nutritious beverage offering many health benefits. It is an excellent source of antioxidants, vitamins, and minerals that are crucial for maintaining a healthy body. This recipe is perfect for people looking for a quick and simple snack or breakfast option that is low in calories and nutrients. The smoothie is particularly beneficial for people who are looking to improve their digestive health, boost their immune system, or manage their weight. It can be consumed at any time of day, but it is especially good in the morning or after a workout. Overall, the Mixed Berry Smoothie Recipe is a great addition to any healthy diet.

Prep Time:5 minutes

Cook time: 1 minute

Total Time: 6 minutes

Serving:2

Ingredients

- 1 1/2 cups of apple juice (if you prefer, also use almond milk, skim milk, coconut milk, or other flavors of juice)
- 1 sliced banana
- 1 1/2 cups of frozen mixed berries
- 3/4 cup of vanilla Greek yogurt
- 1 tbsp of honey (optional)
- Optional garnish: fresh berries and mint sprigs

Instructions

1. Place the apple juice (or other liquid), sliced banana, mixed berries, and vanilla Greek yogurt into a blender.
2. Blend the ingredients until the mixture becomes smooth. If the smoothie appears too thick, you may add a little more liquid, around 1/4 cup at a time.
3. Taste the smoothie and add a tbsp of honey if desired. Blend again to mix well.
4. Pour the mixed berry smoothie into two glasses.
5. Optional: Garnish each glass with fresh berries and mint sprigs.
6. Serve and enjoy your delicious and healthy mixed berry smoothie!

61. ORANGE CARROT GINGER SMOOTHIE

The Orange Carrot Ginger Smoothie is a healthy and refreshing drink that's perfect for anyone looking to improve their overall health. Its combination of fresh carrot, orange, ginger, and frozen fruit is packed with nutrients, antioxidants, and anti-inflammatory properties. Also drinking it first thing in the morning can help your immune system, digestion, and energy levels throughout the day. It's a flawless choice for a quick and easy breakfast or snack that's delicious and nutritious. Whether you're a busy professional, fitness enthusiast, or just looking for a healthy alternative to sugary drinks, the Orange Carrot Ginger Smoothie is a great option.

Prep Time:5 minutes

Total Time: 5 minutes

Serving:1

Ingredients

- 1 large carrot, peeled and sliced
- 1 whole orange, peeled (or a scoop of orange juice concentrate)
- 1 frozen banana
- 1/2 cup of frozen mango or pineapple chunks
- 1 thumb-sized piece of ginger root
- 1 cup of water

Instructions:

1. First, add all of the ingredients into a blender.
2. Blend the mixture until it is smooth and creamy. If necessary, add additional water to achieve the desired level of consistency.
3. Pour the smoothie into a T-shaped glass, and serve immediately. Enjoy!

62. ORANGE CRANBERRY SMOOTHIE

This smoothie packed with vitamin C from the oranges and antioxidants from the cranberries provides a nutritious boost any time of day. The banana adds potassium and fiber to keep you full and satisfied. With no added sugar, this smoothie makes a guilt-free, refreshing treat. Enjoy it for breakfast to start your day energized.

The almond milk provides calcium without the dairy, making this smoothie lactose-free. Blend it up for a mid-morning snack to curb cravings. The maple syrup gives it just a touch of natural sweetness. With the fiber, potassium, and vitamin C, this smoothie supports heart and immune health. So drink up any time of day, and feel good knowing you're giving your body nutrients it needs. It's the perfect pick-me-up!

Prep Time:5 minutes

Total Time: 5 minutes

Serving:2

Ingredients

- 2 large oranges
- 1 cup of frozen cranberries (100 grams)
- 1 large banana
- 1 cup of unsweetened almond milk (250 ml)
- 3 tbsp maple syrup

Instructions

1. Start by peeling the oranges and removing any seeds or white pith.
2. Add the oranges, frozen cranberries, banana, almond milk, and maple syrup to a blender.
3. Blend the ingredients together until smooth and creamy.
4. Taste the smoothie and add more maple syrup if desired.
5. Pour the smoothie into a T-shaped glass and serve immediately.
6. Enjoy your delicious Orange Cranberry Smoothie!

63. ORANGE CREAMSICLE SMOOTHIE

The Orange Creamsicle Smoothie is a sweet and tangy recipe perfect for anyone who wants a healthy and delicious beverage. It's high in sugar and calories, so it's best consumed as an occasional treat in the morning or early afternoon. The smoothie is a great source of vitamins and nutrients and is made with wholesome ingredients like a ripe banana, orange juice, and vanilla Greek yogurt. Overall, the Orange Creamsicle Smoothie is a tasty and refreshing choice for those looking to add more fruit and dairy to their diet.

Prep Time:5 minutes

Total Time: 5 minutes

Serving:2

Ingredients

- 1 frozen ripe banana, previously peeled and sliced
- 2 tsp pure vanilla extract
- 1/2 cup of orange juice
- 3/4 cup of vanilla Greek yogurt
- 1 orange, peeled and sliced
- Optional: 2 tsp orange zest

Instructions

1. Add the frozen banana chunks, vanilla extract, and orange juice in a blender.
2. Blend the ingredients together on high speed until the mixture becomes thick, creamy, and smooth. This should take around 3 minutes. Now scrape down the sides of the blender as required to ensure that all of the components are thoroughly combined.
3. Add the vanilla Greek yogurt, peeled and sliced orange, and orange zest (if using) to the blender.
4. Blend all the ingredients together until everything is combined and the mixture is smooth.
5. Next, taste the smoothie and adjust the sweetness or thickness as needed. If the smoothie is too much thick, add more orange juice or water to thin it out. Now add a drizzle of honey or maple syrup if it is not sweet enough.
6. Pour the Orange Creamsicle Smoothie into glasses and serve immediately. Enjoy your delicious and refreshing smoothie!

64. PEANUT BUTTER AND JELLY SMOOTHIE

Peanut Butter and Jelly Smoothie is a delicious and nutritious drink that is perfect for those who are looking for a healthy and filling snack. Packed with mixed frozen berries, all-natural peanut butter, vanilla protein powder, rolled oats, and milk, this smoothie provides a balanced mix of carbs, proteins, and healthy fats. It is a good source of energy and is perfect for drinking as a breakfast or post-workout drink. This smoothie is also ideal for individuals looking to increase their protein intake or maintain a healthy lifestyle. Drinking it fresh is recommended to get the maximum health benefits.

Prep Time:5 minutes

Total Time: 5 minutes

Serving:1

Ingredients

- 1 cup of mixed frozen berries
- 1-2 tbsp of all-natural peanut butter
- 1/4 cup of vanilla protein powder (any kind)
- 2 tbsp of rolled oats
- 1 cup of milk (any kind)

Instructions

1. Add all of the ingredients into a high-speed blender.
2. Blend the ingredients on high until a smooth texture is achieved.
3. If the smoothie appears too thick, add a little more milk and blend again.
4. If the smoothie is a little too thin, add more frozen berries or rolled oats and blend again.
5. Once the desired texture is achieved, pour the smoothie into a glass.
6. Serve and enjoy immediately!

65. PEACH APRICOT SMOOTHIES

The Peach Apricot Smoothie is a delicious and healthy beverage that is perfect for any time of the day. Packed with the goodness of fruits like peaches, apricots, and banana, this smoothie is a rich source of most needed vitamins and minerals that are essential for good health. The recipe also includes evaporated milk, which adds a creamy texture to the smoothie while keeping it low in fat. This refreshing drink is an ideal choice for people who are looking for a nutritious and filling snack that can be enjoyed on the go or as a meal replacement.

Prep Time:5 minutes

Total Time: 5 minutes

Serving:1

Ingredients

- 1 1/2 cups of (375 mL) frozen peaches
- 1 1/2 cups of (375 mL) Carnation® Regular, 2% or Fat-Free Evaporated Milk
- 1 1/2 cups of (375 mL) apricot or peach nectar or orange juice
- 1 banana, cut in pieces
- 1/4 cup of (50 mL) Smucker's® Pure Apricot Jam
- 1 tsp (5 mL) vanilla extract

Garnish

- Fresh mint leaves
- Peach slices

Instructions

1. Combine frozen peaches, evaporated milk, apricot or peach nectar (or orange juice), banana pieces, apricot jam, and vanilla extract in a blender.
2. Pulse the mixture and then process on high speed until the mixture is smooth.
3. Pour the smoothie into serving glasses.
4. Garnish the smoothie with fresh mint leaves and a skewered peach slice.

66. PEACH COBBLER SMOOTHIE

This Peach Cobbler Smoothie recipe is not only delicious but also a healthy drink that can be enjoyed any time of the day. With the goodness of non-fat Greek yogurt, frozen peaches, old-fashioned oats, and a hint of honey and cinnamon, this smoothie is packed with fiber, protein, and vitamins. It's an ideal drink for people who are looking for a quick and healthy breakfast or snack option.

This smoothie can be enjoyed immediately after blending and is a perfect refreshment for hot summer days. It's a great way to add more fruit and fiber to your diet and stay energized throughout the day.

Prep Time:5 minutes

Total Time: 5 minutes

Serving:1

Ingredients

- 1 (6 oz) container non-fat peach Greek yogurt (such as Simply 100)
- 1 pound frozen peaches*
- 1 tspvanilla extract
- 1/4 cup of old-fashioned oats
- 1/4 tspcinnamon
- 1 tbsp honey (more or less, to taste, depending on the sweetness of the peaches)

Instructions

1. Prepare the frozen peaches: Wash and dry the peaches, cube them, and place them into an airtight container. Freeze overnight.
2. Thaw the frozen peaches in the microwave for 30-60 seconds or until slightly softened.
3. Place all ingredients into a high-powered blender, such as a Vitamix, and blend until smooth.
4. Serve the smoothie immediately.
5. Enjoy your delicious and healthy Peach Cobbler Smoothie!

67. PEACH MANGO GREEN SMOOTHIE

This Peach Mango Green Smoothie recipe is a delicious and healthy way to start a day. Packed with vitamins and minerals from mango, peach, kale, and flaxseeds, this smoothie is perfect for people who want to stay healthy and energetic. Soy milk provides a great source of protein, while kale adds essential nutrients like iron and vitamin C. This smoothie can be enjoyed at any time of day, but it's particularly beneficial as a breakfast or post-workout drink. Overall, this recipe is a great choice for anyone looking to add more fruits and vegetables to their diet.

Prep Time:5 minutes

Total Time: 5 minutes

Serving:3

Ingredients

- 1 peeled and chopped mango
- 1 cup of (250 g) frozen peach slices
- 2 frozen bananas
- 1 cup of (25 g) kale
- 2 cups of (480 mL) unsweetened soy milk†
- 1 tsp (2 g) ground flaxseeds

Instructions

1. Add the mango, frozen peach slices, frozen bananas, kale, soy milk, and ground flaxseeds to a blender.
2. Next, blend all the ingredients together until the mixture is smooth.
3. If you like a thinner consistency, add more soy milk and blend again.
4. Pour the smoothie into a T-shaped glass and serve immediately.
5. Enjoy your Peach Mango Green Smoothie!

68. PEACH RASPBERRY SMOOTHIE

Peach Raspberry Smoothie is a delicious and healthy drink that's perfect for anyone looking for a refreshing and nutritious beverage. Made with frozen peaches, raspberries, milk, yogurt, and honey, this smoothie is rich in antioxidants, vitamins, and minerals that can support overall health and well-being. It's a good source of dietary fiber, which can help in digestion and keep you feeling full for longer. This smoothie is an ideal beverage for breakfast or as a post-workout snack. It's also a great option for people who are looking for a dairy-free alternative to traditional smoothies.

Prep Time:5 minutes

Total Time: 5 minutes

Serving:3

Ingredients

- 1/2 cup of milk (any variety)
- 1/2 cup of vanilla yogurt
- 1 cup of frozen peaches
- 1/2 cup of frozen raspberries
- 1 tbsp honey (or more, to taste)

Instructions

1. Add the milk and yogurt to a blender.
2. Add the frozen peaches, raspberries, and honey to the blender.
3. Blend the ingredients until smooth.
4. If desired, garnish with fresh mint and raspberries.
5. Enjoy the Peach Raspberry Smoothie immediately.

69. PEACHY KEEN SMOOTHIE

Peachy Keen smoothie is a delightful and refreshing drink that's perfect for summer. This smoothie is packed with essential nutrients like Vitamin C, fiber, and potassium, which are vital for maintaining good health. The combination of peaches, bananas, yogurt, and vanilla extract creates a smooth, creamy, and sweet flavor that will leave you feeling satisfied and revitalized. This smoothie is an excellent choice for people who looks for a healthy and nutritious breakfast or snack. It's best to drink this smoothie immediately after blending to enjoy the fresh taste and all the nutritional benefits.

Prep Time: 7 minutes

Total Time: 7 minutes

Serving:4

Ingredients

- 1 cup of peach nectar
- 1 banana, sliced
- 1 cup of peach yogurt
- 2 cups of fresh peaches, sliced
- 1 tspvanilla extract
- 2 tbsp granulated sugar
- 2 cups of ice cubes

Instructions

1. Add all ingredients to a blender.
2. Cover the blender with its lid and blend until the mixture is completely smooth.
3. If the mixture is too thick, you can add more peach nectar or water to thin it out.
4. Once the smoothie is ready, pour it into glasses and serve immediately.

70. PEANUT BUTTER AND BANANA OATMEAL SMOOTHIE

The Peanut Butter and Banana Oatmeal Smoothie is a tasty and nutritious beverage perfect for breakfast or a post-workout snack. Loaded with protein, fiber, and wholesome fats, this smoothie offers lasting energy and contributes to a satisfying sense of fullness.This smoothie is an excellent choice for people with busy schedules or those looking for a quick and easy meal on the go. It's also ideal for individuals trying to build muscle or maintain a healthy weight. Enjoy this smoothie any time of day for a delicious and satisfying treat.

Prep Time: 5

Total Time: 5

Serving:4

Ingredients

- 2 ripe bananas
- 1 cup of low-fat milk (any kind works)
- 1 cup nonfat vanilla Greek yogurt
- 1 cup of old-fashioned oats
- 1/4 cup of natural peanut butter
- 1 tspcinnamon
- 2-3 large scoops of ice (or more to taste)

Instructions

1. Peel the bananas and break them into smaller pieces.
2. Add the bananas, milk, Greek yogurt, oats, peanut butter, cinnamon, and ice to a high-speed blender.
3. Blend all the ingredients on high speed until the mixture is completely smooth.
4. Should the smoothie be overly thick, incorporate additional milk or water to achieve your preferred consistency.
5. Pour the smoothie into glasses and enjoy immediately.

71. PEANUT BUTTER AND JELLY SMOOTHIE

The Peanut Butter and Jelly Smoothie is a delicious and healthy beverage perfect for breakfast or a post-workout snack. Packed with protein from peanut butter, vanilla protein powder, and fiber from rolled oats, this smoothie such perfect way to fuel your body and keep you feeling full and satisfied. It's also a best option for people who are lactose intolerant or in vegan diet, as it can be made with non-dairy milk. However, it's essential to remember that this smoothie is relatively high in calories, so it's best enjoyed in moderation.

Prep Time:5

Total Time:5

Serving:1

Ingredients

- 1 cup of mixed frozen berries
- 1-2 tbsp of all-natural peanut butter
- 1/4 cup of vanilla protein powder (any kind)
- 2 tbsp of rolled oats
- 1 cup of milk (any type)

Instructions

1. Put all the ingredients in a high-speed blender.
2. Blend until a smooth texture is achieved.
3. Pour the smoothie into a glass and savor it!

72. PEANUT BUTTER BANANA SMOOTHIE

Peanut Butter Banana Smoothie is a tasty and nutritious beverage that is ideal for breakfast or as a snack. It's high in potassium, fiber, and protein, making it a perfect choice for a pre-workout or post-workout recovery drink. The smoothie is gluten-free and suitable for people following a vegetarian or vegan diet. However, because of the high calorie and sugar content, this smoothie should be consumed in moderation and as part of a well-balanced diet. Overall, it's a great drink for anyone looking for a pleasant and nutritious beverage.

Prep Time:5

Total Time:5

Serving:1

Ingredients

- 3/4 cup of coconut milk without sugar
- 1 big banana, frozen after being cut up.
- 2/fourths of a cup of smooth peanut butter
- 12 cup of basic nonfat Greek yogurt
- 1/8 tsp of cinnamon powder
- Optional: ice
- Optional mix-ins: 1/2 scoop vanilla or chocolate protein powder, 1 tbsp flaxseed meal, one tbsp chia seeds

Instructions

1. Add the almond milk, frozen banana chunks, creamy peanut butter, nonfat plain Greek yogurt, and ground cinnamon in a blender.
2. Add any optional mix-ins such as vanilla or chocolate protein powder, flaxseed meal, or chia seeds if desired.
3. Blend all ingredients until smooth.
4. Add some ice cubes and blend again if you prefer a thicker consistency.
5. Once blended to your desired consistency, pour the smoothie into a glass and enjoy immediately.

73. PEANUT BUTTER CUP SMOOTHIE

The Peanut Butter Cup Smoothie is a nutritious and delicious beverage ideal for breakfast, post-workout, or as a snack. This smoothie, made with peanut butter, banana, cocoa powder, and milk, is high in protein, fiber, and healthy fats. It's an excellent method to fulfill your sweet taste while still eating a healthy diet. This smoothie is ideal for anybody who likes peanut butter and is looking for a quick, easy meal alternative. On the other hand, those who are allergic to nuts should avoid them. This smoothie is perfect for a nutritious and delicious snack at any time of the day!

Prep Time:5

Total Time:5

Serving:2

Ingredients

- 3 tbsp peanut butter
- One banana, sliced and frozen
- 1 tbsp dark cocoa powder
- 1 tbsp honey
- 1 cup / 240 ml / 8 fl ounce milk (dairy or non-dairy)

Instructions

1. Layer the ingredients in the blender. Add the milk, honey, peanut butter, cocoa powder, and frozen banana slices. Starting with the liquids will help blend the smoothie better.
2. Blend the ingredients until everything is well combined and the mixture is completely smooth and creamy. Depend it on your blender, you may need to pulse a few times to ensure the frozen banana is well incorporated.
3. Check the texture of the smoothie. If it's too thin, add more frozen bananas to thicken it up. To thin it out if it's too viscous, add more milk.
4. If desired, pour the smoothie into glasses and garnish with a drizzle of peanut butter, melted chocolate, and crushed peanut butter cups.
5. Enjoy your Peanut Butter Cup Smoothie!

74. PINA COLADA SMOOTHIE

Pina Colada Smoothie is a refreshing drink made with pineapple, banana, Greek yogurt, coconut milk, and shredded coconut. It is a healthy drink perfect for people looking for a nutritious and delicious beverage. This smoothie is high in vitamins, minerals, and antioxidants, which can improve your health and well-being. It is an ideal drink to have in the morning or after a workout to replenish your energy levels. The Pina Colada Smoothie is perfect for anyone who wants to stay fit, active, and healthy without compromising taste.

Prep Time:5

Total Time:5

Serving:2

Ingredients

- 2 cups of pineapple chunks
- Two frozen bananas
- 1/2 cup of vanilla Greek yogurt
- 2 tbsp shredded coconut
- 1 1/2 cups coconut milk

Instructions

1. Add the pineapple chunks, frozen bananas, Greek yogurt, shredded coconut, and coconut milk to a blender in the order listed.
2. Blend the ingredients quickly for 2-3 minutes until you get a smooth and creamy texture.
3. Sample the smoothie and modify the texture by incorporating more coconut milk if it's too thick, or add a sweetener of your preference if it lacks sufficient sweetness.
4. Pour the smoothie into a glass or mason jar.
5. Serve immediately and enjoy cold or store it in the fridge for 24 hours.

75. PINEAPPLE COCONUT SMOOTHIE

Pineapple Coconut Smoothie is a delicious and healthy drink perfect for anyone who loves tropical flavors. It is made with frozen pineapple chunks, coconut milk, and yogurt, making it a great source of vitamins, minerals, and antioxidants. The smoothie can be enjoyed any time of the day, but it is incredibly refreshing in the morning or after a workout. It is also an excellent option for those following a dairy-free or vegan diet.

Prep Time:5 Min

Total Time:5 Min

Serving:1

Ingredients

- One handful of ice
- 1 cup of frozen pineapple chunks
- 1/4 cup of plain or vanilla yogurt
- 1/4 cup of coconut milk
- 1/4 cup of milk of choice (soy, almond, regular)
- 1/2 tbsp unsweetened shredded coconut

Instructions

1. Add the ice, frozen pineapple chunks, yogurt, coconut milk, and regular milk to a blender.
2. Combine the ingredients and blend until smooth. If the mixture is excessively thick, incorporate one or two tbsp of milk to achieve your preferred consistency.
3. Transfer the smoothie into a glass and garnish with unsweetened shredded coconut.
4. Serve immediately, and enjoy your Pineapple Coconut Smoothie!

76. PINEAPPLE MANGO GREEN SMOOTHIE

Pineapple Mango Green Smoothie is a refreshing and healthy drink ideal for anybody seeking a nutrient-dense lunch on the run. This smoothie is packed with fiber, vitamins, and minerals, making it an excellent choice for overall wellness. This smoothie is best consumed in the morning as a breakfast or post-workout drink. This smoothie is ideal for anybody looking to enhance their general health, particularly those attempting to boost their fruit and vegetable consumption.

Prep Time:5 Min

Total Time:5 Min

Serving:1

Ingredients

- 1 cup of milk as your choice
- 1/2 frozen banana
- 1 cup of chopped mango
- 1/2 cup of chopped fresh pineapple
- 2 cups of fresh spinach or kale
- 1/2 cup of ice

Instructions

1. To a blender, add all the components.
2. Blend until smooth and buttery at high speed.
3. Check to see if the smoothie is too thick, add more milk until it gets the right consistency.
4. Serve the smoothie right away after pouring it into cups. Enjoy

77. PINEAPPLE ORANGE SMOOTHIE

The Pineapple Orange Smoothie is a healthy drink that mixes the sweet flavors of pineapple and orange with the smoothness of Greek yogurt. It is high in vitamins C and B6, calcium, and potassium. This smoothie is ideal for a quick breakfast or a light snack. It is best ingested in the morning to offer an energy boost to start the day. This drink is ideal for anybody searching for a nutritious and delicious drink, particularly those who are health-conscious and often on the go.

Prep Time:20 Min

Total Time:20 Min

Serving:3/4

Ingredients

- 2 cups of frozen pineapple chunks
- 1/2 cup of orange juice
- 1/2 cup of milk (soy milk or almond milk can also be used)
- One container (5.3 oz.) of pineapple-flavored Chobani Greek Yogurt

Instructions

1. To a blender, add all the components.
2. Blend until smooth and buttery at high speed.
3. Check to see if the smoothie is too thick. If it is, add more milk until the right consistency is reached.
4. Serve the smoothie right away after pouring it into cups. Enjoy!

78. PUMPKIN PIE SMOOTHIE

Pumpkin Pie Smoothie is a wholesome and pleasant drink that may be had at any time of day. Thanks to the pumpkin puree, almond milk, and yogurt, it's high in nutrition, and it's spiced with cinnamon, ginger, and nutmeg. This smoothie is ideal for anybody seeking a healthy, seasonal drink with pumpkin pie flavor. It's also a good alternative for people who wish to eat more plant-based cuisine. Anyone allergic to nuts should avoid using almond or pecan butter in this recipe.

Prep Time:10 Min

Total Time:10 Min

Serving:1

Ingredients

- 1 frozen banana
- ½ cup of plain or vanilla yogurt
- ½ cup pumpkin puree
- ½ cup of unsweetened almond milk
- 1 tbsp almond or pecan butter
- 1 tspvanilla extract
- ½ tspground cinnamon
- Pinch each of the nutmeg, ginger & allspice

Instructions

1. To a blender, add all the components.
2. Blend until buttery and smooth.
3. Add more almond milk progressively until you reach the desired consistency if the smoothie is too thick.
4. Pour into glasses and enjoy your delicious pumpkin pie smoothie!

79. PUMPKIN SPICE LATTE SMOOTHIE

The Pumpkin Spice Latte Smoothie is a delicious and healthy way to experience the tastes of autumn. This smoothie's pumpkin puree and bananas are high in fiber, vitamins, and minerals. Greek yogurt contains enough protein to keep you satisfied for longer. The smoothie may be drunk at any time of day, although it is ideal as a breakfast or mid-morning snack. It's perfect for anybody searching for a tasty and nutritious way to start their day or fuel their exercises. Those lactose intolerant should replace a non-dairy option with Greek yogurt.

Prep Time:5 Min

Total Time:5 Min

Serving:2

Ingredients

- 2/3 cup of pumpkin puree
- 1/2 cup of canned full-fat coconut milk
- 1/2 cup of Greek yogurt
- 1/4 cup of almond milk (or more to thin to desired consistency)
- 2 bananas, quartered and frozen
- 6 cold brew coffee cubes* (or substitute ice cubes + 2 tsp instant coffee)
- 1 tsppumpkin pie spice
- 1/4 tspground ginger, pinch of ground nutmeg

Instructions

1. Add all the ingredients to a blender.
2. Process the mixture until it's smooth and creamy.
3. If you want a thinner consistency, add in additional almond milk.
4. Enjoy the smoothie by pouring it into a tumbler.

80. RASPBERRY COCONUT SMOOTHIE

A delightful drink made with frozen raspberries, coconut milk, agave syrup, and cardamom, Raspberry Coconut Smoothie. This smoothie is high in vitamins and minerals, making it nutritious. It is ideal for individuals who want to enhance their digestion, strengthen their immune system, and enjoy a tasty drink. The smoothie can be a snack or breakfast beverage, and it is ideal for hot summer days. It is crucial to mention that anyone allergic to nuts should avoid coconut milk.

Prep Time:5 Min

Total Time:5 Min

Serving:2

Ingredients

- 2 cups of (250g) frozen raspberries
- 3/4 cup of (180 ml) coconut milk
- 1/3 cup of (80 ml) water, or more if needed
- 1 to 2 tbsp agave syrup
- 1 pinch of freshly ground cardamom (optional)*

Instructions

1. Reserve two raspberries for decoration, and add the remaining frozen raspberries and coconut milk to a blender.
2. Blend the ingredients until you get a smooth texture.
3. If desired, add the agave syrup and a pinch of cardamom, and stir everything together.
4. Add more water until the smoothie has the required consistency if it is too thick.
5. Transfer the mixture to the refrigerator and allow it to cool for at least one hour.
6. Once chilled, pour the smoothie into a glass and decorate it with two reserved raspberries.
7. Enjoy your delicious Raspberry Coconut Smoothie!

81. RASPBERRY LEMONADE SMOOTHIE

Raspberry Lemonade Smoothie is a healthy and pleasant drink with frozen red raspberries, nonfat Greek yogurt, almond milk, fresh lemon juice, and pure maple syrup. This smoothie is high in fiber, antioxidants, and probiotics, making it an ideal drink for improving digestion, strengthening immunological function, and aiding weight loss. It is best suited for persons who desire a nutritious and low-calorie drink that can be enjoyed anytime. Those with diabetes, on the other hand, should exercise caution while consuming pure maple syrup, which is heavy in sugar.

Prep Time:5 Min

Total Time:5 Min

Serving:1

Ingredients

- 1 cup of frozen red raspberries
- 4 ounces of nonfat Greek yogurt
- 1/4 cup of almond milk
- 1 tbsp fresh lemon juice
- 1 tbsp pure maple syrup
- Red raspberries for garnish

Instructions

1. Add the frozen red raspberries, nonfat Greek yogurt, almond milk, fresh lemon juice, and pure maple syrup to a blender, or use a handheld immersion blender.
2. Process the ingredients until the mixture is smooth and creamy.
3. Pour the raspberry lemonade smoothie into a glass.
4. Garnish the smoothie with more red raspberries.
5. Serve and enjoy the refreshing and healthy smoothie.

82. RASPBERRY LEMONADE GREEN SMOOTHIE

The Raspberry Lemonade Green Smoothie is a light and pleasant drink that may be enjoyed at any time of day. This smoothie is packed with nutrients from kale, raspberries, and flax seeds and is terrific for increasing energy and promoting general health. Adding lemon adds a zesty bite, while prunes or dates can be added for sweetness. It is ideal for individuals who want to boost their diet of fruits and vegetables and can be used as a snack or meal replacement. Due to the high fiber level, persons with digestive difficulties should exercise caution.

Prep Time:5 Min

Total Time:5 Min

Serving:1

Ingredients

- 1 cup of frozen raspberries
- 3/4 cup of water (or more, depending on desired thickness)
- 2 tbsp ground flax seeds
- 1 tbsp sesame seeds
- 4 leaves of kale, stalks removed
- 1/2 fresh lemon, peeled
- 2 prunes, pitted and soaked, or 2 tbsp REAL prune butter
- Optional: additional pitted prunes or dates for desired sweetness.

Instructions

1. In a blender, combine the frozen raspberries and water. Pulse the frozen berries in the water before blending until smooth.
2. Add the ground flax and sesame seeds to the blender and blend until combined.
3. Add one kale leaf at a time and blend well. If you are new to green smoothies, start with one or two leaves.
4. Blend in the peeled lemonAdd the soaked, pitted prunes or prune butter to the blender and blend until smooth.
5. Taste the smoothie and add other pitted prunes or dates for desired sweetness.Serve the Raspberry Lemonade Green Smoothie chilled, and enjoy!

83. RASPBERRY MANGO SMOOTHIE

Raspberry Mango Smoothie is a light and cheerful drink that may be enjoyed at any time of day. This smoothie is high in vitamins, minerals, and fiber, which can help with digestion, immunity, and weight loss. It is also suitable for persons who are lactose intolerant or follow a vegan diet. The chia seeds in the smoothie give omega-3 fatty acids, while the honey adds sweetness. This smoothie is best consumed in the morning for breakfast or as a snack to help satisfy hunger and keep you energized throughout the day.

Prep Time:5 Min

Total Time:5 Min

Serving:1

Ingredients

- 1 cup of fresh mango, diced
- 1/2 cup of fresh raspberries
- 1 frozen banana
- 1/3 cup of unsweetened almond milk
- 1/2 tspof chia seeds
- 1 tspof honey

Instructions

1. Add the mango, raspberries, frozen banana, almond milk, chia seeds, and honey to a blender.
2. Mix everything together until it is creamy and smooth.
3. Add more almond milk if the drink is too thick.
4. Put the smoothie in a glass and start drinking it right away.

84. RASPBERRY PEACH COCONUT SMOOTHIE

Raspberry Peach Coconut Smoothie is a simple and refreshing drink that may be had at any time of day. This smoothie, made with frozen peaches, raspberries, orange juice, coconut milk, and honey, is high in vitamins, minerals, antioxidants, and fiber. It is appropriate for people searching for a nutritious and tasty beverage alternative, and it may be enjoyed as a breakfast, snack, or post-workout drink. On the other hand, those who are allergic to nuts should avoid coconut milk as an alternative.

Prep Time:5 Min

Total Time:5 Min

Serving:1

Ingredients

- 1 slightly-rounded cup of frozen, sliced peaches
- 1/2 cup of frozen raspberries
- 1/2 cup of orange juice (freshly squeezed is extra delicious)
- 1/2 cup of canned coconut milk (light can be used; milk of your choice can also be substituted)
- 2 tsp honey, or to taste (sweetener of your choice may be substituted)
- 1/8 tspcinnamon
- Optional: extra raspberries for garnish

Instructions

1. Place the frozen peaches, raspberries, orange juice, canned coconut milk, honey, and cinnamon in a blender.
2. Blend all the ingredients until completely smooth.
3. Pour the smoothie into two 8-ounce glasses or one 16-ounce cup. Mason jars also work well as containers.
4. Add a few extra raspberries to the smoothie as a garnish if desired.
5. Serve and enjoy your Raspberry Peach Coconut Smoothie!

85. RASPBERRY PEACH SMOOTHIE

Raspberry Peach Smoothie is a healthy drink with frozen raspberries, fresh peaches, Greek yogurt, and almond milk. It is best suited for those who want a low-calorie, nutrient-dense drink. Smoothies are great summer drinks that you can drink at any time of day. It will taste and feel best if you drink it right after you make it. It has a lot of vitamins, minerals, and antioxidants, so people who want to boost their immune system should eat it.

Prep Time:5 Min

Total Time:5 Min

Serving:2

Ingredients

- 1 cup of frozen raspberries
- 3/4 cup of fresh peaches, chopped
- 1/4 cup of vanilla Greek yogurt
- 1/3 cup of vanilla almond milk

Instructions

Add all the ingredients to a blender, with the liquid ingredients (vanilla almond milk and vanilla Greek yogurt) first.

Blend the ingredients on high speed for 2 minutes or until the mixture is completely smooth.

Put an end to the mixer and clean the sides. Blend again for 30 seconds to make sure all the ingredients are well mixed.

Put the smoothie in a glass and start drinking it right away.

86. RASPBERRY WHITE CHOCOLATE SMOOTHIE

This Raspberry White Chocolate Smoothie is a beautiful and nutritious way to start your day or satisfy your sweet appetite. It's packed with antioxidants and nutrients from raspberries and Greek yogurt, making it ideal for people searching for a nutritious and enjoyable snack or meal replacement. The addition of white chocolate chips adds a sensual touch. Perfect for everyone who likes a sweet and fruity treat. Eat it any time of day, but keep the calorie count in mind if you're managing your consumption.

Prep Time:5 Min

Total Time:5 Min

Serving:1

Ingredients

- 1 tbsp of white chocolate chips
- 1 container (approximately 2/3 cup) of raspberry Greek yogurt
- 3/4 cup of frozen raspberries
- 3/4 cup of milk of your choice

Instructions:

1. Heat the white chocolate chips in a small microwave-safe bowl for about 30 seconds until they are melted and smooth. Stir until there are no lumps and set aside to cool slightly.
2. Add all ingredients into a high-speed blender, including the melted white chocolate.
3. Then combination should be blended until it is creamy and smooth. You can add more milk to smooth out the mixture if it is too thick.
4. Pour the raspberry white chocolate smoothie into a glass and enjoy it immediately!

87. SPICED APPLE SMOOTHIE

A spiced Apple Smoothie is a delicious and healthy beverage that can be enjoyed anytime. It's a source of protein and nutrients from Greek yogurt and almond or coconut milk. The frozen apple provides a refreshing and sweet taste, while the apple pie spice adds a warm, comforting flavor. This smoothie is perfect for a healthy, tasty, and easy-to-make drink. It's also an excellent option for breakfast or as a post-workout snack.

Prep Time:5 Min

Total Time:5 Min

Serving:1

Ingredients

- 6 ounces of plain Greek yogurt
- 1 cup of almond or coconut milk
- 1 frozen apple, diced and seeded
- 1 tspvanilla extract
- 1/2 tspapple pie spice
- 1-2 tbsp sweetener (optional), such as agave, sugar, or xylitol

Instructions

1. Add all ingredients to a blender.
2. Blend it until it's smooth.
3. Check, if the smoothie is too thick, add more milk to thin it out.
4. Pour into a glass and enjoy immediately.

88. SPICED MANGO SMOOTHIE

A spiced Mango Smoothie is a healthy and delicious drink that can be enjoyed anytime. This smoothie is an excellent source of vitamins and minerals, including vitamin C, which helps to boost the immune system. Combining ginger, cardamom, and turmeric provides anti-inflammatory and digestive benefits. The smoothie is perfect for vegans and people who are lactose intolerant. It is also a refreshing and energizing drink for anyone looking for a quick and easy way to increase their daily fruit intake.

Prep Time:5 Min

Total Time:5 Min

Serving:2

Ingredients

- 2 cups of silk unsweetened coconut milk
- 1 cup of silk peach mango soy dairy-free yogurt alternative
- 2 tbsp fresh lemon juice
- 1/4 tsp ground cardamom
- 2 cups of frozen mango chunks
- 1 tsp minced ginger
- 1/8 tsp ground turmeric
- 1 tbsp pure maple syrup (optional)

Instructions

1. Add all the ingredients to a blender.
2. Mix everything together until it is smooth and creamy.
3. If desired, add more maple syrup for sweetness.
4. Pour into glasses and serve immediately.

89. STRAWBERRY BANANA SMOOTHIE

Strawberry banana milkshake is a tasty and healthy drink that you can drink any time of day. Packed with nutrients from fresh fruit, Greek yogurt, and milk, it's a great source of vitamins, fiber, and protein. This smoothie is perfect for anyone looking for a quick and easy way to add more fruits to their diet. It's also an excellent option for breakfast or as a post-workout snack. However, people with lactose intolerance or dairy allergies should avoid this recipe or use non-dairy milk and yogurt substitutes.

Prep Time:5 Min

Total Time:5 Min

Serving:2

Ingredients

- 2 cups fresh strawberries, washed, hulled, and halved
- 1 banana, peeled, sliced into quarters, and frozen
- 1/2 cup of Greek yogurt
- 1/2 cup of milk

Instructions

1. Wash, hull, and halve the strawberries. Peel the banana and slice it into quarters. Freeze the banana quarters for at least 2 hours or overnight.
2. Add the frozen banana quarters, halved strawberries, Greek yogurt, and milk to a high-powered blender.
3. Blend the ingredients on high until completely smooth and creamy, occasionally stopping to scrape down the sides of the blender with a spatula.
4. Pour the smoothie into the cups and serve right away. Enjoy!

90. STRAWBERRY BASIL SMOOTHIE

Strawberry Basil Smoothie is a refreshing and healthy drink with fresh strawberries, Greek yogurt, basil leaves, and honey. It's an excellent choice for a quick breakfast or post-workout snack. This smoothie suits anyone seeking a low-calorie, high-nutrient drink packed with vitamins and minerals. Enjoy it in the morning or as a mid-day pick-me-up.

Prep Time:5 Min

Total Time:5 Min

Serving: 4

Ingredients

- 1/2 cup of fresh strawberries, washed and hulled
- 10 fresh basil leaves, washed and cut into strips
- 1 tbsp honey
- 2/3 cup of Greek yogurt

Instructions

1. Wash the strawberries and remove the green tops. Cut the strawberries in half.
2. Wash the basil leaves and cut them into thin strips.
3. Place the strawberries, basil leaves, honey, and Greek yogurt into a blender.
4. Blend the mixture until it's smooth and frothy.
5. Pour the juice right away into a glass and serve.

91. STRAWBERRY MANGO SMOOTHIE

Strawberry Mango Smoothie is a healthy and refreshing drink with frozen strawberries, mango, carrots, almond milk, and lemon juice. It has a low amount of calories and fat and is a good source of vitamins, minerals, and antioxidants. This drink is great for people who want to eat well or lose weight. It's also a good choice for a drink before or after a workout. You can have this drink for breakfast in the morning or as a snack during the day. Be careful not to drink it too late at night, because the natural sugars in it may keep you awake.

Prep Time:3 Min

Total Time:5 Min

Serving:2

Ingredients

- 2 cups of frozen strawberry slices
- 1 1/2 cups of frozen mango pieces
- 1/2 cup of carrots or baby carrots, chopped
- 1 1/2 cups of almond milk or milk of your choice, plain, plus more as needed
- 1 tbsp of freshly squeezed lemon juice or 1/4 cup of freshly squeezed orange juice. If you use orange juice, lower the amount of almond milk to 1 1/4 cups.

Instructions

1. First, add all of the ingredients to a blender: frozen strawberries, frozen mango, chopped carrots, almond milk, and lemon juice.
2. Blend the ingredients until smooth. If the mixture is too thick, add almond milk as needed to reach your desired consistency.
3. Pour the smoothie into glasses and enjoy immediately.

92. STRAWBERRY PINEAPPLE SMOOTHIE

This delicious Strawberry Pineapple Smoothie is a refreshing and healthy drink, perfect for any time of day. It's packed with nutrients from fresh fruits and can be boosted with optional add-ins such as protein powder or collagen. This smoothie is excellent for anyone looking for a healthy beverage option, whether for breakfast, a snack, or a post-workout. It's also a perfect way to increase fruit intake for those who struggle to eat enough fruits throughout the day.

Prep Time:5 Min

Total Time:5 Min

Serving:2

Ingredients

- 8 oz. vanilla almond milk (or regular milk, or orange juice)
- 2 cups of frozen strawberries
- 2 cups of fresh pineapple chunks (canned is delicate)
- OPTIONAL AD-INS
- 1 scoop vanilla protein powder
- 1 scoop collagen
- a splash of vanilla extract
- a splash of lemon juice

Instructions:

1. Place the almond milk (or regular milk or orange juice), frozen strawberries, and fresh pineapple chunks (or canned pineapple) in a blender.
2. Blend the ingredients until smooth.
3. Add one or more of the ad-ins listed above (vanilla protein powder, collagen, vanilla extract, or lemon juice) and pulse until combined.
4. Spoon the smoothie into two 12-16 oz. Glasses.
5. Serve and enjoy your refreshing Strawberry Pineapple Smoothie!

93. STRAWBERRY SHORTCAKE SMOOTHIE

The Strawberry Shortcake Smoothie is a delicious and healthy drink that can be enjoyed anytime. Made with frozen strawberries, unsweetened almond milk, Greek yogurt, and butter extract, this smoothie is low in calories and protein. It's an excellent choice for those looking for a quick and nutritious breakfast or a post-workout snack. It's also suitable for vegetarians and those with gluten-free diets. Enjoy it immediately after blending for the best taste and texture.

Prep Time:5 Min

Total Time:5 Min

Serving:1

Ingredients

- 1 cup of frozen strawberries
- 3/4 cup of unsweetened almond milk
- 1/2 cup of vanilla Greek yogurt
- 2 tsp butter extract

Instructions

1. Add the frozen strawberries, unsweetened almond milk, vanilla Greek yogurt, and butter extract to a blender.
2. Blend all ingredients quickly until the mixture is smooth and reaches the desired consistency.
3. Check, if the smoothie is too thick, add more almond milk and stir until it reaches the required consistency.
4. If the smoothie is too watery, add more frozen strawberries or ice to the blender until the right consistency is reached.
5. Pour the juice right away into a glass and serve. Enjoy your Strawberry Shortcake Smoothie, it tastes great!

94. STRAWBERRY WATERMELON SMOOTHIE

The Strawberry Watermelon Smoothie is a refreshing and nutritious drink perfect for those looking for a healthy and delicious beverage. It's packed with vitamins, antioxidants, and other essential nutrients that promote overall health and well-being. Drinking it in the morning or as a snack in the afternoon is best. This smoothie is perfect for anyone looking to improve their diet and add more fruits to their daily intake, especially those who follow a vegan or vegetarian diet.

Prep Time:2 Min

Total Time:2 Min

Serving:2

Ingredients

- 10 ounces frozen strawberries
- 3 cups of fresh watermelon chunks

Instructions

1. Add the frozen strawberries and fresh watermelon chunks to a high-powered blender.
2. Blend the mixture until it becomes smooth, creamy, and uniform in texture.
3. Once the smoothie is ready, pour it into serving glasses.
4. Serve immediately and enjoy your refreshing and delicious Strawberry Watermelon Smoothie.

95. SWEET POTATO SMOOTHIE

Sweet Potato Smoothie is a nutritious beverage that is rich in vitamins C and A, potassium, and fiber. It is perfect for those looking for a healthy and filling breakfast or snack option. The ginger and turmeric in this smoothie can help with inflammation, and the addition of hemp hearts provides a boost of protein. It is suitable for anyone looking to add more vegetables to their diet, and it's best to drink it in the morning or as a post-workout recovery drink.

Prep Time:10 Min

Total Time:10 Min

Serving:1

Ingredients

- 1/2 cup of cooked sweet potato, packed
- firmly
- 1 quart almond milk (or milk of your choice)
- 2 to 3 sliced Medjool dates
- 1/2 inch raw ginger knob (or 1/4 tspdried ginger)
- 1/4 tsp turmeric powder
- 1/4 tsp cinnamon
- powder
- 1 heaping teaspoonful hemp hearts (optional; for added protein)
- As required, ice to thicken

Instructions

1. Blend the sweet potato, milk, 2 dates, ginger, turmeric, cinnamon, and hemp hearts in a mixer.Blend the ingredients until it is very smooth.
2. If more sweetness is required, add another date to the mixture.
3. Add a heaping cup of ice cubes and blend until thoroughly broken down once smooth. If you want a thicker shake, add more ice, but bear in mind that more ice will dilute the overall flavor.
4. Serve immediately cold

96. TROPICAL SUNRISE SMOOTHIE

Tropical Sunrise Smoothie is a healthy and refreshing drink that can be enjoyed anytime. Best suited for those who want to boost their immune system and add variety to their diet. It contains vitamin C, fiber, and healthy fats from coconut milk. Drink it immediately after blending to get the most nutrients.

Prep Time:5 Min

Total Time:5 Min

Serving:1

Ingredients

- 2 oranges
- 1/2 pear
- 1/2 cup of vanilla-flavored coconut milk

Instructions

1. Peel the oranges and remove any seeds.
2. Cut the pear into small pieces and remove the core.
3. Place the oranges, pear, and coconut milk in a blender.
4. Blend all the ingredients on high speed until smooth and creamy.
5. Pour the juice right away into a glass and serve.

97. VANILLA BERRY SMOOTHIE

Vanilla Berry Smoothie is a delicious and healthy drink perfect for people who want to increase their protein intake while enjoying berries' sweet and tangy flavors. It can be consumed at any time of the day but is especially significant as a post-workout snack. This smoothie is low in calories, antioxidants, vitamins, and fiber, making it an excellent choice for weight-conscious and health-conscious individuals.

Prep Time:5 Min

Total Time:5 Min

Serving:2

Ingredients

- 1 ½ cups of water (360 mL), or yogurt or milk of choice
- 1 scoop vanilla protein powder
- 1 cup of frozen strawberries (150 g)
- 1 cup of frozen blueberries (100 g)
- ½ cup of frozen raspberries (60 g)
- ½ cup of frozen blackberries (75 g)

Instructions

1. Add all ingredients to a blender.
2. Mix everything together until it is smooth and creamy.
3. If the mixture is too thick, add more water or milk until it reaches your desired consistency.
4. Pour into a glass and enjoy your delicious Vanilla Berry Smoothie!

98. VANILLA CHAI SMOOTHIE

Vanilla Chai Smoothie is a healthy and flavorful beverage that's perfect for anyone looking for a nutritious and delicious drink. The combination of almond milk, Greek yogurt, and chai tea provides protein, calcium, and antioxidants. The smoothie is also sweetened naturally with maple syrup or honey, making it a great alternative to sugary drinks. It's ideal for breakfast, a snack, or a post-workout drink. However, it's important to note that individuals with lactose intolerance or allergies to nuts should avoid this recipe.

Prep Time:5 Min

Total Time:10 Min

Serving:1

Ingredients

- 1 cup of almond milk
- 2 chai tea bags
- 1/2 cup of Greek yogurt
- 1 tbsp maple syrup or honey
- 1/2 tspvanilla extract
- 1/4 tspChai Spice or cinnamon

Instructions

1. Pour almond milk into a microwave-safe coffee mug and microwave on 50% power for 1 1/2 to 2 minutes.
2. Steep the chai tea bags in almond milk according to the package instructions.
3. Let the chai tea cool to room temperature or chill it in the fridge for 15 minutes or overnight.
4. Combine the cooled chai tea, Greek yogurt, maple syrup or honey, vanilla extract, and Chai Spice or cinnamon in a blender.
5. Blend until smooth.
6. If you want to, you can pour the drink into a glass and decorate it with more Chai Spice or cinnamon.
7. Enjoy your Vanilla Chai Smoothie!

99. VANILLA HONEYDEW SMOOTHIE

The Vanilla Honeydew Smoothie is a refreshing and healthy drink for those seeking a nutrient-rich beverage. It's a great source of vitamins and minerals, thanks to honeydew and spinach. Adding fat-free vanilla Greek yogurt gives it a creamy texture and some protein, while lime juice adds a zesty flavor. This smoothie is perfect as a snack or breakfast drink and can be enjoyed by anyone looking to improve their overall health.

Prep Time:5 Min

Total Time:5 Min

Serving:2

Ingredients

- 2 cups of chopped honeydew
- 1/2 cup of spinach
- 1/2 cup of fat-free vanilla Greek yogurt
- 1/2 cup of milk
- 1 tbsp lime juice
- 1/4 cup of ice cubes

Instructions

1. Throw everything into a blender.
2. Mix the ingredients until they are smooth and fluffy.
3. Pour the smoothie into a glass.
4. Garnish the smoothie with some honeydew.
5. Serve and enjoy your delicious Vanilla Honeydew Smoothie!

100. VANILLA MATCHA SMOOTHIE

The Vanilla Matcha Smoothie is a delicious and healthy beverage that combines antioxidant-rich matcha powder with the natural sweetness of bananas and a hint of vanilla. It's perfect for those looking for a caffeine boost without the jitters, and the recipe can be easily adjusted to suit personal taste preferences. This smoothie is best consumed in the morning as a breakfast replacement or pre-workout drink. It's also an excellent option for anyone who wants to incorporate more plant-based and dairy-free options into their diet.

Prep Time:5 Min

Total Time:5 Min

Serving:2/3

Ingredients

- 2 frozen bananas
- 1 cup of original Almond Breeze Almond Milk
- Matcha powder, a few tsp to a few tablespoons.
- A tiny scrape from about 1-inch of a vanilla bean pod
- A few handfuls of ice
- Honey, agave, or sweetener of choice (optional)

Instructions

1. Add the frozen bananas, Almond Breeze Almond Milk, matcha powder, vanilla bean scrape, and ice to a blender.
2. Blend the ingredients until smooth.
3. Taste the smoothie and adjust the sweetness according to your liking by adding honey, agave, or your preferred sweetener.
4. Put the smoothie in a glass and start drinking it right away.

Printed in Great Britain
by Amazon